KARDEC'S SPIRITISM

Also by Emma Bragdon

*Spiritual Alliances: Discovering the Roots of Health
at the Casa de Dom Inácio*

*The Call of Spiritual Emergency:
From Personal Crisis to Personal Transformation*

*A Sourcebook for Helping People
with Spiritual Problems*

The cover and symbol for this book:

The dandelion is a common plant indigenous to Europe,
Asia, Africa and North America. It is extremely hardy, with-
standing frost, and capable of seeding itself in many areas.
Its leaves are a rich source of vitamins and minerals. It can
be used medicinally, and the flowers can be used to make a
delicious wine. It also benefits from being picked.

Dandelions can turn a springtime meadow, awakening from
winter, into a radiant sea of gold. The dandelion is an agent of
transformation and knows how to transform itself. It changes
from a yellow gold flower with many small petals united to its
stem, to a globe of white, feathery seeds, which eventually
detach, and blow away in the wind to establish new plants.

Who is not fascinated by the sphere of delicate seeds of the
dandelion, in its last hours of holding close to the stem, before
letting go to be transported by the breeze? What a delight to
hold the dandelion, at seed stage, blow the seeds into the air,
and watch them find their way.

Still, the dandelion is classified as a weed.

KARDEC'S SPIRITISM:

A Home for Healing and Spiritual Evolution

Emma Bragdon, PhD.
Director: Spiritual Alliances, LLC.
Woodstock, Vermont, USA.

Foreword by
Rustum Roy, PhD.
Chairman: Friends of Health
Member: U.S. National Academy of Science

Lightening Up Press
Woodstock, Vermont

Published by:
Lightening Up Press
PO Box 325
Woodstock, VT. 05091, USA
802-457-4915

Prepublication copies distributed only through July 1, 2004, by:
Enfield Books and Distribution
603-632-7377
info@enfieldbooks.com

After July 1, 2004 Copies Available on Amazon.com
ISBN#0-9620960-5-9

Prepublication: March, 2004

Bragdon, Emma, 1946-
Kardec's Spiritism: A Home for Healing and Spiritual Evolution
Includes bibliographic references, glossary, and index.
1. Spirituality 2. Metaphysics 3. Health 4. Religion 5. Brazil

Graphic Illustrations and Cover Design:
Marty Cain (marty@nhvt.net)

Graphic Design and Typography:
Cookson Desktop Publishing (mark.cookson@valley.net)

Printing:
R.C. Brayshaw & Co, Inc. (www.rcbprinting.com)

Table of Contents

Acknowledgement   i
Foreword by Rustum Roy, PhD.   iii
Introduction   vii
        The US Health Care System
        Kardecist Spiritist Centers Can Help

PART ONE

THE NATURE OF "KARDECISMO"   1

Chapter One: 3
        What is a Kardecist Spiritist Center?
        Seminal Ideas—Structural Foundation
        The Typical Kardecist Center
        A Home for Energy Medicine
        A Resource We Neither Have Nor Recognize

Chapter Two: 17
        The History
        Demographics
        Historical Perspective
            Hippolyte Rivail/Allan Kardec
            Kardec's Spiritism Comes to Brazil
            Today's Leadership
            A Personal Note

Chapter Three: 29
        Sorting Out Spiritism vis a vis Spiritualism and Religion
        Comparing Spiritism and Spiritualism
        Is Spiritism a Religion?
        A Map of Spiritual Evolution

Chapter Four: Supporting Personal Spiritual Evolution   37
The Levels of Spiritual Evolution
Physical
Emotional
Mental
Integrated Personality
Levels of Initiation
The Faculties of the Spiritual Man or Woman
New Groups/New Religions

PART TWO

PORTRAITS OF CONTEMPORARY CENTERS   53

Chapter Five: Palmelo   55
Medical Intuition
Dis-Obsession and De-Possession
Marcel's Schizophrenia
From Mental Illness to Mediumship
The Place and the People

Chapter Six: Busca Vida   67
Marlene's Cancer Treatment
Laussac's Electromagnetic Devices
Replacing Energy Passes
Vital to All Healing

Chapter Seven: The Centro   79
Tania: Preventive Medicine
Cleide and Her Son: Confronting Cancer

Chapter Eight: The Brazilian Federation of Spiritists
        of San Paulo (FEESP)   89
Help for the Addict
Elsie: Becoming a Leader

PART THREE

**BUILDING BLOCKS OF SUCCESSFUL
KARDECIST SPIRITIST CENTERS**   95

Chapter Nine: Financial and Human Resources   97
　　The Organizational Structure
　　Managing Financial Resources
　　　　Raising Money
　　　　Allocating Money for Expenditures

Chapter Ten: Classes and the Preparation of Teachers   103
　　The Basic Course
　　After the Basic Course: Further Study
　　Training for Mediumship
　　Training to Give "Energy Passes"
　　Preparation of Teachers
　　Finding Teachers Outside Brazil

**Chapter 11: First Steps Toward Creating a
　　　　　　Spiritist Center In Your Town**   121
　　Fraternity and Fraternities
　　First Steps in the USA
　　Personal Note
　　Restrictions and Successes
　　Summary

Notes   125

Glossary   137

Appendix One:
How Christianity Relates to the Concept of Reincarnation   145

References and Suggested Reading   157

Index   165

List of Diagrams:
The Spiritual Path/ The Path of Materialism   35-36
The Path to Abnormal Cell Growth   71

Acknowledgements

I deeply appreciate the generosity of Laurance Rockefeller and the Lloyd Symington Foundation who sponsored the research and printing of this book.

I have had the great good fortune to come to know Elsie Dubugras and Martha G. Thomaz, two women who have been leaders in the development of Kardecist Spiritism in Brazil since the 1940s. I have learned much from their wisdom, good humor, and dedication to the path of service. Julika Kiskos, a Brazilian psychologist, both introduced me to these leaders, and helped me understand Spiritism through the lens of Parapsychology. She took Spiritism "out of the clouds of mysticism" and anchored it into the footprint of science, as her teacher, Hernani Andrade, did.

I thank other wonderful Brazilians who also gave of their time and goodwill to help me gather details about Spiritist Centers in Brazil and the philosophy behind their good works. Without the friendship of Elizabeth Pereira, of Abadiania, this book could not have been created.

Johann Grobler, MD, is one of those avant-garde psychiatrists who integrates notions intrinsic to the path of spiritual evolution into his practice of medicine. Since we met in March, 2001, our conversations have helped refine my thinking on many themes articulated in this book. Johann has also been my host and benefactor allowing me to visit his Lighuis (Lighthouse) Farm in South Africa, and use his extensive library during three long retreats. Johann's analysis of Laussac's electromagnetic medical devices grounded and supported my enthusiasm for this new arena of Energy Medicine.

My community of friends and sources of spiritual guidance, stretching all around the world, continue to bring peace, good humor, and inspiration into my life. The interconnectedness we share inspires me to work with joy.

The ferocity, friendship and caring of my editor, Joby Thompson, is the reason this book is as cogent as it is. Profound thanks.

May this book honor the Perennial Wisdom teachings, the teachers, and all loving beings who inspire us to proceed on the "Path of Love."

January, 2004
Woodstock, Vermont
and
Lighuis Farm, South Africa

i

Foreword by Rustum Roy, PhD.

In his 2003 Presidential Address to the AAAS (American Association for the Advancement of Science), Floyd Bloom, Professor of Neuroscience at U.C. San Diego and former Editor of "*Science*," minces no words. Nor can anyone else who calls himself or herself a scientist mince words any longer. Bloom introduces the paper thus: "This problem is the imminent collapse of the American health care system." He refers to "the Delusions of Success" of the incredibly expensive research system for medicine. ($25 billion of public funds for NIH alone ... $1 billion of private money to bring *one* new major drug to market.)

Emma Bragdon's book offers a practical, down to earth, thoroughly researched (i.e. studied, with ample reproducible data), possible partial solution to the U.S.' problems. Unbelievable you say!? . . . well, read it first. As a physical scientist holding five professorships in three Universities, elected to the National Academies of the U.S. and four major countries, and one who has intensively studied the field of Whole Person Healing (much superior in accuracy, as a title, to CAM-complementary and alternative medicine) for some years, I must say that some aspects of Bragdon's suggestion are much more likely to stay the collapse of the U.S. system than ANY research, ANY breakthrough, ANY gadget that our dominant high-tech paradigm can produce. More gas in the tank, or a new battery, or repaired tires, have nothing to contribute to helping your car find its way in a strange city. This is a long way to say: This book is extremely relevant and important to the future of American health care.

When I read about and watched various videos, and talked to friends whom we sent down to visit the Brazilian Abadiania Spiritist center, and studied the incontrovertible scientific data, I came to the same puzzled states that Bragdon describes. How is it possible that the American public, the American medical establishment, and U.S. policy makers are totally (100%) ignorant of these completely inexorable facts.

As a physical scientist, working by science's rules, not those of medical research, to me the facts were absolutely clear. In literally millions of cases, the experiences of "psychic surgery" consistently broke the Western paradigm: surgery was performed routinely in the open air in crowded rooms with no anesthesia, no pain, no bleeding, no sepsis; day in and day out. Obviously our Western paradigm is simply wrong or perhaps inadequate. I then recalled the wisdom of a very politically savvy and practical scientist, Benjamin Franklin. He wrote: "You will observe, with concern, how long a useful truth may be known and exist, before it is generally received and practiced on." That is where the United States stands today, being forced by economic realities perhaps, to now receive the truth of Bragdon's observations, and begin to shape their own practices in accord with it.

The reader gets several excellent, concise introductions in Emma's book. First the history via which Allan Kardec, the French intellectual, influenced a whole Portuguese colony by the practices of his disciples. Second, both the agreed upon general principles and the differences among the different Spiritist centers and practitioners. Third, Dr. Bragdon's very insightful treatment of the commonalities of "theory" among the diversities of "practice" among different brands of centers. I believe that Bragdon's treatment here is both subtle and nuanced. First and foremost as she states "Spiritual healing may ultimately be more important than bodily healing." All of the energized world community now emerging under the banner of "Whole Person Healing" recognize that the key error of allopathic medicine was the single-minded focus on a person as a 'Body' alone. Kardecists, Spiritists, (and all whole person healers) simply state the obvious when they assert that Spirit matters, and profoundly so in health. While Bragdon struggles with the distinction between spirituality and religion (as many theologians are doing today), she ultimately comes down on the correct etymological definition of religion. Re-ligio is indeed to bind again, to re-connect, via practice. All true religions affirm both theory (belief) and experience (practice). 'Faith' and 'works' are hardly a novel idea in all traditions. The Spiritist tradition links belief and practice at the point of the most universally experienced need—for health. The vast majority in the Christian world today simply have forgotten (or never knew) that Jesus was basically a well-known healer. Moreover, his spiritual insights were passed on in profoundly situational ways, for each individual to learn from their own responses. The vagabond son returns and the father rejoices and kills the fatted calf. The stranger in the ditch needs help. No dogma—only practice—but deeply connected to the spirit of caring and its translation into action.

Bragdon carefully dissects the non-sectarian, yet profoundly spiritual nature of the culture of Brazil in which all this occurs. I myself have puzzled over the question: Can the Spiritist experience be duplicated in the U.S.? I believe it works in Brazil (and say the Philippines) because these Catholic cultures are deeply steeped in belief in the reality of the spiritual realm or dimension, *not* the details of Catholic dogma. Bragdon points out how universally ecumenical (with respect to "dogma") all these centers are. In that respect, they presage the future of all other cultures. But there the relations diverge. Our "advanced"(?) Western culture has (only) in the last fifty years become for the first time in human history a **culture of disbelief**. There is no coherent mythos, no belief structure, which unifies this culture. If a culture lacks a unifying re-binding together (a religion) can it be a culture at all?? Is "Western culture 2004" an oxymoron? But Bragdon's book is aiming deeper: to provide the "blueprint" as she calls it—for starting a center for the study and practice of Spiritist healing. I heartily endorse the concept, albeit only to provide a channel for accepting reality for our dogmatist, reductionist, body-only practitioners.

Relevant to this Foreword is the challenge in Bragdon's book. How can we not start a center to study and disseminate widely what is learned about these Spiritist Centers. It may help our health care system, but even more importantly it may help our whole culture of disbelief.

Rustum Roy, PhD.
January, 2004
Chairman: Friends of Health
www.rustumroy.com

Introduction

I n the Spring of 2001 I visited a Kardecist Spiritist Center, called the Casa de Dom Inácio, in Abadiania, Brazil. It was my first experience of *"Kardecismo"*— a spiritual community center patterned after life principles compiled by Allan Kardec (1804 -1869), from channeled teachings. His books are written to help us live by principles that accelerate personal spiritual evolution and healing.

David Hess, an anthropologist, professor, and author, wrote two books[1] about Kardec's Spiritism. He sums it up this way: Kardec's doctrine includes beliefs that we associate with esoteric traditions (the astral body, vital fluids, and spirit communication through mediums), East Indian philosophy (reincarnation and karma), reformed Protestant theology (the interpretation of heaven and hell as psychological states), Catholicism (emphasizing spiritual hierarchies who gain position through their stage of spiritual purity), social reformism (emphasizing equality, progress, freedom of thought and education); as well as modern science (parapsychology, metaphysics, the new physics, and the study of subtle energy applied to healing).

A wonderful outline of the philosophy, but Hess did not fully acknowledge the way it has been translated into action. In the following pages you will read about the effectiveness of Kardec's centers. The healing being done, charity being given, and education for life being shared, all of which suggests ways we can improve our own system for health management.

Some Centers have kept general records summarizing how many people have been helped with each service provided and what the success rate is in helping people recover from drug or alcohol addiction. A hospital administrator who teaches classes at the Brazilian Spiritist Federation in San Paulo claims they have a 95% success rate in helping addicts recover from dependency on drugs or alcohol[2]. When you read about Centro in

Chapter Seven, you will read that 87% of people attending that Center claim to receive measurable healing of physical conditions ranging from minor pain to cancer. 70% report great improvement, or a cure. This information was published in a nationally circulated Brazilian magazine, Planeta, in April, 2002[3]. Of course, these statistics are very meaningful and encourage anyone interested in health and healing to take a closer look at what makes Kardecismo so effective.

Approaching my first visit to a rural Kardecist Center in Brazil, the Casa de Dom Inácio in Abadiania, I expected to encounter some archaic rituals. Things that, while they may be interesting, could also be difficult for a Westerner to identify with. Since I don't speak fluent Portuguese, I also expected I would have some difficulty in understanding what I was seeing.

What I saw was clear and simple. It also amazed me—this center is not only addressing the universal needs of today, it is more successful, in many ways, than the resources for health management we have in the "first world." People were healing from cancer and AIDS as well as from psychological diseases, like schizophrenia and manic-depressive disorder—illnesses that modern mainstream medicine is not always capable of curing[4]. In addition, the consultations and surgeries that resulted in this healing at the Casa are *free*. The treatments are, for the most part, non-invasive, pain-free and generate no infection. While not every individual experiences a full remission of symptoms (perhaps because their degenerative disease is too far progressed), most visitors have profound spiritual experiences. That means, they have what can only be described as an experience of communion with Powers, such as God or angels, that brings comfort and peace of mind.

After publishing "*Spiritual Alliances: Discovering the Roots of Health at the Casa de Dom Inácio*" to document the work of John of God, I continued to visit Brazil, exploring other centers, and meeting more people who have been healed.

In October, 2003, I met Beth, a lawyer from Brasilia. She had been fully healed of two medical problems at a Spiritist center in Palmelo. I was especially impressed by her story of cure from ovarian cancer. The healing took one week of rest and seclusion in an inn, where she was from time to time given spiritual healing by visiting mediums. Her brother, unable to function in normal life, diagnosed in his twenties as schizophrenic, also came for treatment to the same center. Now, more than twenty years have gone by. Since being treated this man has no psychotic symptoms, maintains a healthy, stable, intimate relationship with his wife, enjoys sharing parenting their children, and works fulltime. These kinds of healings rarely occur in the USA.

The US Health Care System

Don't we have the best in health care? That assumption is often made. Here are the facts:

- The US, compared to other nations, ranks #37 in effectiveness of health care according to a United Nation's World Health Organization (WHO) study conducted in June, 2000.

- After more than three decades and a trillion research dollars, an American succumbs to cancer every single second of the day. J.C. Bailar, MD, PhD, from Harvard University addressed the Vice President's Cancer Panel Meeting this way: "I conclude that our decades of war against cancer have been a qualified failure."

- According to the Journal of the American Medical Association (JAMA), April 14, 1998, more than 290 people die each day from adverse reactions to FDA approved drugs—more than three times the number of deaths caused by automobile accidents. In 2000, JAMA reported there are almost a quarter million deaths per year caused by medical errors and adverse reactions to FDA approved drugs. *This makes our own medical system the third leading cause of death after heart disease and cancer.* [5]

- In 1997 it was estimated that side effects from prescription drugs cost our nation 78 billion dollars.[6]

We have the most expensive health care system in the world (about one trillion dollars per year, one fifth of our gross national product—but *only our emergency medical care ranks first in quality.* In June, 2000, the WHO found Japan leading the world in "healthy life expectancy," with the USA at #20, falling behind every country in Europe as well as Canada, Australia, and Israel. The infant mortality rate in the USA is higher than that in many struggling countries, for example, the number of infants who died before their first birthday is 13.3 per thousand in New York City, but 10.9 in Shanghai. [7]

Although our needs in the United States are of less magnitude than those in the poorest third world countries, e.g. some countries in Africa where over 30% of the population has AIDS, we all are caught in a similar dilemma of needing to find economical, effective health care. The poor and uneducated, everywhere, are not getting sufficient support. People with chronic illnesses and degenerative disease, such as AIDS, are marginalized, unless they can afford to pay for special support services. They do not have the resources for medicine or food, and governments are often not organized to adequately help them. The gap between the wealthy and the poor is vast.

Former Congressman Berkley Bedell, Chairman of the Board at the National Foundation for Alternative Medicine writes, "Over forty three million people in the USA cannot afford health insurance; healthcare has almost become a luxury item. Globally, over five billion people can not afford prescription medications. The need for affordable health solutions is largely ignored in our current medical paradigm which has created a system of medical care that is unsustainable." [8]

"The performance we receive for what we invest in health care is probably the biggest failure in American History."
— Business Week, August 26, 2002

In his book, "*Power versus Force*," Psychiatrist David Hawkins writes, "The health care industry is so overburdened with fear and regulation that it can barely function. Healing from individual illness or the healing of the health care industry itself can only occur by the progressive steps of elevation of motive and abandonment of self-deception, to attain new clarity of vision. There are not any villains; the fault is in the misalignment of the system itself. If we say that health, effectuality and prosperity are the natural states of being in harmony with reality, then anything less calls for internal scrutiny rather than the projection of blame on things outside the system involved.[9]"

The health care system in America is in trouble. Former Assemblyman from the New York State Legislature (1970-1976), Dan Haley, writes, "...the US has one of the most bureaucratically controlled and over-regulated medical systems in the world." [10] ..."we don't have a free market in non-toxic therapies in the US—in things that, by definition, can't hurt us."[11]... "the FDA clamped upon the US a harsh regime of censorship and repression of anything that could compete with the giant drug companies." [12]

Our health care system needs an overhaul. However, the 'internal scrutiny' that Hawkins advocates takes precious time, and making decisions to change the system, to foster effective, non-toxic therapies, also takes time. Meanwhile, according to JAMA in 1998,[13] 55% of our population and 83% of cancer patients are trying new forms of complementary and alternative health care, usually paying out of pocket. There is a dramatic rise in visits to alternative practitioners — from 427 to 629 million — nearly double the 386 million visits to primary care physicians. In answer to consumer demand, many clinics and hospitals, are now creating entire departments dedicated to complementary health care, e.g. Memorial Sloan-Kettering Cancer Center in New York City, and Myrna Brind Center at Thomas Jefferson Hospital in Philadelphia.

"Where the people lead, the leaders must follow." — Ghandi

However, most of our research dollars are still dedicated to exploring the efficacy of prescription drugs. The conventional medical field seems to thwart efforts to develop affordable healthcare.[14] The National Foundation for Alternative Medicine, started by former congressman, Berkley Bedell, writes, that it takes at least five years to clinically document the effectiveness of a new therapy; meeting the requirements of the Food and Drug Administration generally takes one billion dollars for one new drug or treatment protocol; the National Cancer Institute budget for cancer research is over $4 billion; the scientists at the National Institutes of Health have refused to test most alternative therapies, even ones that show promise for humans.

"There are reasons why doctors ignored non-Western treatments for so long. Most of the alternative or complementary therapies like massage therapy or herbal remedies can't be patented. And since no one's going to make a lot of money from them no one wants to finance their investigation."

—Barrie Cassileth, PhD.
Memorial Sloan Kettering Cancer Center

Two-time Nobel Prize winner Dr Linus Pauling put it bluntly: "The war on cancer is largely a fraud." Why? Little research money is devoted to complementary medicine, if they are protocols that cannot be patented, e.g. herbal remedies. Clinical trials for complementary health protocols that are low-cost, effective, and originate in an entirely different paradigm than the conventional bio-chemical, rarely get funded.

Kardec's Spiritist Centers Can Help

Spiritist Centers offer a model, a way out. They should, at least, be part of the conversation about finding a remedy to our situation.

For the poor, they offer free medical consultation, nutritional supplements, and medication, to those who prove need. They can respond to needs more quickly than our slow-moving, bureaucratic systems of welfare, e.g. Medicare and Medicaid in the USA. As reported in *Newsweek*, our medical researchers now recognize that both mental and physical health are improved through involvement in community, through volunteer work, and spiritual activities like prayer and meditation.[15] Spiritist Centers create a place for those activities under one roof, thus providing a baseline of physical sustenance, improved health, preventive care for illness, allaying the costs of managing sickness, and contributing to spiritual wellness and evolution.

People who regularly attend church have a 25 percent reduction in mortality—that is, they live longer—than people who are not churchgoers.
— Dr. L. H. Powell, Rush University Medical Center[16]

Preliminary data on a trial of 750 heart patients shows that 30% had lower death rates if they were prayed for and given a special program of music, therapeutic touch and guided imagery.
— Dr. Mitchell Krucoff, Duke University[17]

People are recognizing that there is a spiritual component to being healthy, and healing. 84% of Americans think that praying for the sick improves their chances of recovery[18]. Many are looking for a way to develop spiritually, not sure where to turn, and concerned with how to maintain a meaningful connection to community. In Brazil, some of these individuals have found their way to Kardecist Centers where they take training to become healers, take classes to study Kardec's philosophy, and learn about spiritual dimensions within an ecumenically-based, caring community. Hopefully in the future we will see the Gates Foundation, or another similar foundation born of corporate profits, sponsoring the maintenance of Spiritist Centers in the USA. In the meantime, if there are not sufficient funds to start a Center, one can certainly consider bringing components of Kardecist Spiritist Centers into our already existing health centers—to revitalize and improve the emotional and spiritually-based therapies.

In Portraits (Part Two), you will be introduced to rejuvenation devices that appear to be highly effective in the tradition of Spiritist healing. Rustum Roy, who wrote the Foreword for this book, told me that our foremost scientists are researching just such electromagnetic devices,[19] and finding they have great potential for healing. They will soon be reviewing the efficacy of such devices in use at Spiritist Centers. In the future, after adequate clinical trials, these apparatuses may also be approved for use in our health maintenance systems and hospitals.

For the patient, it is challenging and sometimes frightening to seek medical help now. "Should I go with conventional treatment, with complementary care, or spiritual healing?" Even though 55%, *more than 116 million North Americans are actively pursuing good health through alternative health care options*, they are usually finding their way without professional guidance, in spite of their doctor's opinion. We need proven paths of alternative health care options. We need blueprints for clinics and health centers that have effectively made these options available. We need doctors and patients to be open to new options, and working together as an aligned team to solve health problems. I hope this book will serve such a purpose.

My intention is to stimulate more research dollars flowing to alternative health protocols, and offer a fascinating sphere of seed thoughts about healing. These seeds can illuminate important alternatives for health, and spiritual growth. My hope is these may sprout into real human centers of personal transformation and healing for individuals and communities, and/ or enhance already existing centers.

Personal Note

I chose to write this book, for the most part, as a reporter. However, I have been so personally moved by what I have discovered in visiting these Centers, it seems also important to include a personal note, from time to time, sharing with you a sense of my subjective experience to give more dimension to the subject.

Having spent a year at the Casa de Dom Inácio, during numerous visits, my personal approach to health and healing has changed radically. I now consider that spiritual healing and spiritual evolution, are more important than physical healing, or curing. Although I would still consult a physician for his/her diagnosis, if I became ill, I would also consult a medical intuitive for both diagnosis and treatment suggestions. Although my preference is to live a long life, I feel more focused on accomplishing the mission I am here to complete, and less attached to the length of this lifetime. Holding on to physical life for as long as possible is not as important to me, as doing 'what I came here to do'. Like many others visiting Spiritist Centers, I have also gone further into letting go of my fear of death. Numerous personal spiritual experiences have convinced me that "death" does not exist. What we call an ending, in death, is but a transition into another form, where the spirit lives independent of the body.

My limited Portuguese did not inhibit my getting tremendous benefit from my visits to Spiritist Centers in Brazil. They speak a language that transcends cultural differences. Through my personal search in Brazil I feel I have come to a much deeper understanding of the word "health" and the components of what we call "healing."

On another note: there are very few clinical trials quantifying the results people have gleaned from their participation in healing activities at Spiritist Centers. This was at first distressing to me. I wanted to see objective statistics on who was coming, when, why, and what the results were. However, I have come to understand and respect the Centers' persistence in maintaining the anonymity of their visitors. You will also understand why, as you read on.

The plethora of anecdotal first-hand stories given to me by international visitors and Brazilians gave me ample reason to believe that extraordinary healing was, and is taking place in these Centers. Also, even if we put measurable physical statistics aside, there is much to learn, of great value, from what is not so easily measured, e.g. the presence of love, a person's sense of leading a meaningful life, and the feeling of well-being. These are also indicators of wellness that we need to bring into our health care systems.

May all sentient beings be happy and at peace.
May we all discover the joy of service and brotherhood.
May we all find a way to carry seeds of new life to the
    ground where they can be a source of nourishment.

PART ONE

The Nature of "Kardecismo"

Kardecismo is the Portuguese term encompassing the way of life, the philosophy, the history and the community centers that are Kardecist Spiritism.

Chapter One

What is a Kardecist Spiritist Center?

Kardecist Spiritist Centers function like alternative health care centers, community centers, and ecumenical schools for spiritual development—all wrapped into one. The list goes on. Looking from various perspectives, call them a grassroots welfare system, a place to study metaphysics, a growth center, an 'after-church' school that transmits values and reflects on universal truths, a social group, a spiritual healing center, a soup kitchen, a free clinic, and a place to cultivate psychic abilities and mediumship. The end goal is spiritual evolution for all.

Walk around and you will see people lined up, waiting for a class to begin, or waiting for their turn with a healer; teachers hurrying to their classrooms, visitors buying books at the bookstore, doctors attending newborns in a private consultation room, interviews being conducted with people entering for the first time, adults enjoying a coffee break together, teenagers sitting in a circle, laughing and talking with a teacher in a classroom, administration going about the business of managing the organization, and staff managing buildings and grounds. The welcoming scent of vegetable soup and fresh bread is in the air.

Currently, there are 6,500 Spiritist Centers throughout Brazil. At least a third of all Brazilians acknowledge the existence of these centers and may visit one or more, as needed. They are places to be healed of physical, spiritual, and psychological maladies of all kinds. This includes cancer, and AIDS, among other less devastating conditions.

Brazilians call Spiritism, "a way of life" that evolved out of recognizing certain universal principles, found in perennial truths that reflect on the forces affecting and controlling the life of man. These universal principles relate him to his environment and the rest of the universe. They present practical principles to live by.

Although all Kardecist Centers share the same philosophy, I found a rich diversity in how Spiritism is lived out in Brazil today. It seems to depend, in large part, on the individuals who manage the centers, and the needs of the people whom they attend. Spiritist centers can be built around either a single, charismatic medium, like John of God, or a small number of people who provide the funding, labor, and leadership of the center.

One common element is found in them all: The people who attend them have a certainty in the presence of God that is extraordinary, and that certainty provides fertile ground for extraordinary healing. The healers treat all who come, irrespective of age, cultural, religious, or socio-economic differences. People seeking healing wait patiently for the attention of the mediums and healers who, it is believed, transmit healing energy from beneficent spirits. The rich wait their turn, sometimes for hours, next to the poor. A sixty-year-old paraplegic waits his turn next to a baby with lymphoma. As they wait, everyone, healers and people coming for healing, pray together—with the intention of evoking the presence of God and the host of disincarnate beings whom, they believe, want to help humans become healthier.

Spiritist Centers in Brazil are started and managed by regular, everyday people, like you and me. They are 'grassroots' efforts, wild in the sense that there is no established form, predictable and stable in the sense that they abide by laws of nature, e.g. every action has an effect, positive actions have positive consequences. These Centers are sustained by a spiritual truth: we are all brothers and sisters. They radiate the love of interconnectedness. The people serve the people. Money necessary to maintain the services and the buildings is donated by people—not churches, not government, and not politicians.

Seminal Ideas—Structural Foundation

Although the philosophy of Kardec will be described in more detail in the next two parts, the beliefs which have led to structural components of the all Kardecist Centers are briefly described below.

The belief in reincarnation, once an intrinsic part of Christian belief (see Appendix A for details) is considered a fact. Also, they believe there are other dimensions where disincarnates, spirits not in body, can be contacted. Spirits, just like human beings, are in the process of evolution. Each spirit lives on in a progression of lifetimes, alternating between life in a body and life in the spirit world, towards the goal of "perfection." This is a state of being defined by wisdom, discernment, ethical behavior, discipline, and pure motivation to serve others. Highly developed spirits, those closer to perfection, can be of great service to human beings in body. Several activities at Spiritist Centers assist people to acknowledge and be in greater contact with these beneficent spiritual beings, to accelerate spiritual evolution.

Spiritism recognizes universal truths and principles to live by that continue from life to life and between lives. For example, the way one interacts with others has inevitable consequences. What you sow, you shall reap. Be kind to others, and they will more likely be kind to you. Be hostile with others, and they will more likely be unkind to you. I hardly ever heard Brazilian Spiritists use the word "karma," but their understanding of the relationship between thoughts, words, and actions and their consequences, cause and effect, certainly resonates with the sacred texts from the Far East on the nature of karma. As in the Far East, Spiritists believe the effects of karma pass through successive lifetimes.

Spiritists believe every person is a medium (a person with a unique way of perceiving and establishing connection to dimensions of life outside the range of our five sense perceptions).

Each person has one or more ways of perceiving the worlds (sacred and profane) beyond the five senses of touching, hearing, tasting, smelling, and seeing. One person may have the gift of "medical intuition"—sensing the pathways of life energy in another person, even though it is imperceptible to the physical eyes, being able to accurately perceive medical problems without objective diagnostic screening. Another person may have dreams that are premonitions of future events, or a palpable sense of the presence of spirits, or God. These gifts can be cultivated to be of service to one's community as well as the fulfillment of one's personal mission on earth. Thus, one person can provide non-invasive, inexpensive medical diagnosis. The next may be able to contact the departed and deliver messages from relatives who have passed on, a comfort to those left behind.

Spiritists have defined over one hundred and twenty kinds of paranormal gifts or powers. Any person may have one or more of these. When harnessed properly, these gifts take one into closer relationship with God. Those who are gifted have the opportunity to spend years developing their gifts in classes for mediumship.

Mysticism: the art of establishing a conscious relationship with the Absolute.
— defined by Evelyn Underhill

Although each individual has unique abilities, it is preferred that healers and mediums work in teams, rather than alone:

Most Spiritist Centers do not focus attention on one or two charismatic leaders who have special gifts of healing or mediumship. In fact, most Centers prefer to have the healers work in teams, to avoid individual ego inflation. The most well developed healers know, as John of God says, "It is not I, but God who does the healing." Still, working in groups, makes it easier for healers to avoid the slippery territory of taking too much pride in "personal" successes. In this way, every success belongs to the group. Every challenge and every disappointment is also born by the group.

Anonymity is assured.

There are no records kept identifying members by name, or of, what diseases each has, or by how much each person donates to the Center. What forms of social assistance each person is using, or has used, is a record kept by the recipient, not the center.

On the other hand, some centers keep general records, keeping count of how many people come for each kind of social assistance, and how many of them are helped.

All activities at the center are free.

No one is asked or expected to make a donation or pay a fee for services received. In fact, it is understood: that which has been freely received from God, should be freely given. Thoughts of money do not have a place in the direct experience of one's connection to the Divine. It follows, then, a healer or medium, expects to be paid, he/she has dropped away from the fullness of direct connection to the realms of spirit.

> "Your intentions must remain pure. You work to be of service, for love. When you work alone, it is easier to lose your ethical standards, get greedy, or get lost in the glamour."
>
> — Elsie Dubugras, Spiritist Leader, in conversation

Spiritual development involves discipline and perseverance, but it does not have to be boring. The community life is punctuated by social events.

Celebrating birthdays, having special meals together, like a "pizza night," or marking national holidays, like Christmas and New Year's Eve, strengthen the bonds of community. People of all ages come together to exchange jokes, play music, eat, dance and sing.

The Typical Kardecist Center

The typical Kardecist Spiritist Center is comprised of one or more modest buildings, with large numbers of folding chairs that can be moved around open rooms, to accommodate diverse numbers of people for different activities.

Wall decorations are usually sparse, and limited to inspirational phrases, or a collection of religious symbols from diverse religious traditions, suggesting an ecumenical theme. A lit candle, a natural crystal stone, flowers, and/or a book on some aspect of Spiritism often rest on a central table.

In a Spiritist Center, everyone is on the same level, everyone wears ordinary street clothes. What is essential to each individual is essential to the whole group: All of us are in the process of growth. Each one of us is capable of personal connection with the Divine. At the same time, each person is unique and has a specific role to play.

Activities include:
- Personal interviews: When a visitor wants to participate in the activities of the center, he/she is asked to have an interview, to identify needs. This gives the Center the opportunity of facilitating each individual in using the Center's resources to full advantage. Individuals

in need are asked to continue to see their interviewer at regular intervals. This prevents the possibility of individuals being overlooked or lost in the crowd.

- Meditation: sitting in silence, to receive spiritual guidance, and to go beyond the chatter of ordinary mental activity and increase awareness of the bonds of love, linking all parts of life.

- Prayer: although the Christian "Lord's Prayer" is frequently recited out loud, people use prayers they have learned from diverse religious traditions, or created for themselves. All prayers are welcome.

- Laying-on of hands, called "energy passes" in Brazil, are available at specific times of the week. The healer/mediums, standing or sitting in a circle around the patient, direct beneficial energy to the body of the patient, without touching him/her. The healer/mediums often amplify the power of the energy being transmitted by focusing together, e.g. sending a stream of green color to an area of the body to stimulate healing.

- A special kind of healing for emotional disorders, to liberate oneself from obsessions and compulsions. This "dis-obsession," or "de-possession," is also accomplished through specific kinds of energy passes. In this case, the healer is helping to separate the patient from a dis-embodied, negatively-motivated spirit, aka "entity," that has become attached to him/her, to free both entity and patient so each can proceed on the path of spiritual evolution.

- Personal consultations with one or more medical intuitives: specific hours of the week are set aside for individuals to receive diagnostic sessions where problems are identified and a treatment plan is suggested. Disease states are usually not identified using medical terminology addressing the symptoms. It is understood that disease states start in the subtle energy body and therefore the roots of illness must be treated in the subtle body, before symptoms in physical organs and systems can be stopped.

- Witnessing "automatic writing." Mediums write messages from the departed to answer questions previously submitted by participants in the assembly. It is thought that the mediums are capable of hearing the transmissions of spirits, and accurately writing what is dictated to them, without distorting it in any way. The messages thus given to people who have lost loved ones can be a great comfort and source of consolation. They again feel the bonds of loving connection connecting the visible to the invisible worlds, reassuring them that passing on out of this life is only a passing to a new kind of life, where they may be reunited with loved ones who have passed on.

- Blessing water to be used to empower healing. Just as energy passes stimulate healing in people, energy can be transmitted by healer/mediums to vitalize water, empowering it for use in healing. This water is used as an antibiotic as well as a way to purify and strengthen the body, mind, and spirit.

- Basic courses give participants an opportunity to discuss universal ideas and principles for living. These classes are designed to orient the student toward the notion that this life is for the purpose of spiritual evolution. Participatory dialogue is essential. Classroom dialogue centers on the expression of values such as compassion and kindness—values stressed in all religions. Texts used to initiate discussions are from Allan Kardec and Chico Xavier, both of whom are said to have collected dictations from highly evolved spirits.

- Courses are also available in practical skill building. These cover: how to conduct an interview with someone who needs social assistance, how to help someone contemplating suicide or confronting addiction, and how to do energy passes for various kinds of healing.

- Training advanced students in classrooms to learn how to use their unique sensibilities as mediums. Texts by Kardec and others are studied along with experiential skill building closely supervised by developed mediums. This skill building continues as student healer/mediums at different levels of development work together in groups attending to those in need coming to the Center for healing.

- Doing charitable work: cooking, serving meals, and giving boxes of food to the destitute; sewing clothes for distribution to the poor; doctors and other professionals volunteering their time, giving free medical, legal, and financial advice to those who can not afford it; distributing nutritional supplements, and medications (only when pre-scribed by a physician on staff).

- A library and/or a bookstore which make books on all aspects of Spiritism available to buy or borrow.

- Art and/or music expositions

The FEB (Federation of Brazilian Spiritists) is the leading national federalizing body for Brazilian Spiritism. FEESP (Federation of Spiritists in the State of San Paulo) is its largest center, but the main offices of FEB are in Brasilia, Brazil. Those that are satellites of FEB, like FEESP, are more authoritarian and bureaucratic than those not part of FEB. Each state has a federation, and has a voice in the FEB's national federative council. FEB controls the council. There have been steps to democratize the FEB further. Alternative visions have sprouted new Spiritist centers, not affiliated with the FEB. Aliança, a loose knit group of independent centers, is one of these.

A Home for Energy Medicine

"The fundamental premise of Western science is wrong because it sets our physical selves against our Souls. It tries to solve problems through technology wars in which the body becomes a battle zone. We wage war on can-cer but forget that healing involves biological creativity, a state of love and compassion... *We have lost our memory of wholeness.*"

— Deepak Chopra, MD. speaking at the
Campaign for Better Health, October, 2003

Jim Oschman, PhD., the author of *Energy Medicine: The Scientific Basis* wrote me a personal note about his field, "Energy Medicine uses dif-ferent forms of energy, such as sound, light, heat, electricity and magnet-ism to stimulate healing. The "Laying-on of Hands" described in the Bible is an ancient form of energy medicine that involves one person using their biological energy field to stimulate healing in another person."

Recent research in biophysics and cellular biology gives us evidence that all living things are essentially energetic systems—that energy is more fundamental than biochemistry. Sophisticated technologies have recently been developed that measure the energy fields within and around living systems. "These *fields of life* have the properties that sensitive individuals have been describing and using for healing for thousands of years, properties that science had long thought did not exist." [1]

The bio-chemical model of the body would have us believe that we are like a bag of water and minerals separated from the environment by the sack of skin that covers us. Change the chemical composition of what is inside this inland sea, extract what is causing pain, and you change the health of the person. In this paradigm drugs and surgery are the most important medical interventions for health maintenance. This model has proven very successful for emergency and trauma medicine, but has not proven nearly as effective in the treatment of degenerative disorders, chronic pain, emotional disturbance, and cancer.

The Energy Medicine model suggests that our cells and our body are essentially energy, not separated from the external environment, but constantly interacting with it. Both internal and "external" energies interpenetrate, and sometimes compete for dominance. Invisible electromagnetic energy in the form of radio waves, microwaves, electric energy from high power lines can disturb, even pollute, the flow of energy and information intrinsic to maintaining homeostasis in the body.

Oschman writes: ..."Oscilllating magnetic fields are being researched at various medical centers for the treatment of bone, nerve, skin, capillary, and ligament damage. Virtually identical energy fields can also be detected around the hands of suitably trained therapists....Research documenting that these different approaches are efficacious is mutually validating. Medical research and hands-on therapies are confirming each other." [2]

We now have machines that give us a graphic picture of energy emanations of various parts of the body. For example, SQUID stands for "Superconducting Quantum Interference Device," an instrument that can calibrate the bio-magnetic field produced by a single heartbeat, muscle twitch, or pattern of neural activity in the brain. Doctors and scientists using the SQUID can see the beginnings of physical disease states in the energy emanations of the body, *prior to any symptoms appearing in the physical body*. Thus, the SQUID is an excellent diagnostic device. These and other measuring devices allow us to proceed with treatments that can prevent the manifestation of disease states.

Using the SQUID, we can immediately see the improvement in the energy system of a patient, brought about by transmission of energy from healers to the patient's bio-electrical field, or the use of specific electromagnetic healing devices for pain management and rejuvenation. Increasingly more data like this demonstrates that treating the body through transmission of energy to both the subtle and physical body allows a health practitioner to work with the roots of health problems. With continued research we may soon establish that using energy for healing is sometimes more effective than bio-chemical protocols (surgery and drugs, that seldom touch the roots of the problem, but only attend to the symptoms).

The SQUID and other refined technologies that measure subtle energy are opening up vast new potentials for effective diagnosis and treatment[3]. In Brazil, Europe and Russia, where governmental certification of devices for energy medicine has been completed, we can see energy medicine in action. Certainly healers at Spiritist Centers are doing just that work when they perform energy passes, or use electromagnetic devices that replace energy passes (see Part Two). Thus, Kardecist Centers are in some significant ways, demonstration centers for contemporary health care protocols being advanced by Biophysics and Cellular Biologists.

The importance for Energy Medicine to find a rightful home is highlighted by Frank Lawlis, MD, an author of the textbook *Mosby's Alternative and Complementary Medicine: A Research Based Approach (2001)*. Lawlis suggests "Energy Medicine may well be "the medicine of the future." He was referring to both the use of electromagnetic devices and spiritual healing. In his chapter on "Electromagnetic Medicine" he writes,

"Bio-electromagnetic medicine applications offer the possibility of more economical and more effective diagnostics and new noninvasive therapies for medical problems, including those considered intractable to conventional treatments. Electromagnetics can provide a better understanding of the fundamental mechanisms of communication and regulation at levels ranging from intracellular to organismic. Improved knowledge of fundamental mechanisms of electromagnetic field interactions could directly lead to major advances in diagnostic and treatment methods....*It may be the most important next step in medical care since antibiotics.*"

Seeing how a Spiritist Center brings these effective Energy Medicine health protocols to the public, can help us better understand how we can create a home for Energy Medicine in our part of the world. Our hospitals, formed on the paradigm of a biochemical model of health management, are slow to encourage the development and use of such new paradigms of health care.

A Resource We Neither Have Nor Recognize

The only thing that bears any resemblance to a Kardecist Center in the USA is Hospice— and a few schools in the USA people are trained to be healers or strengthen particular psychic abilities, such as the Barbara Brennan School of Healing. But, these organizations offer only a small fraction of the resources and services offered at a Brazilian Spiritist Center. At Hospice volunteers help individuals during their transition out of the body into the next dimension. There is compassionate care for the dying and their families, but no classes on principles to live by, managing psychic abilities, or ways to provide laying-on of hands or healing. Unlike Spiritist Centers where no payment is expected, Hospice generally works on a sliding scale, expecting payment when patients and their families can afford it.

Let's reflect a bit more on our resources in the USA: Where do you go if you want spiritual inspiration and simultaneously to be an active member in a community oriented toward spiritual evolution? You may go to a monastery or a convent, but then you may have to sacrifice your relationship to a town or city in order to join a religious community. If you go to a conventional church or synagogue, you must take on a creed. If you don't want to assume a creed, you might go to a personal growth center, take a seminar in comparative religion, perhaps a course or a retreat to immerse yourself in meditation or yoga? You could join a prayer group in your church or travel to a spiritual teacher who has no religious affiliation. In days gone by, people usually chose their churches. Today we have other alternatives, but these are often transitory events, and do not provide a stable, on-going community.

It certainly appears that we have needs that could be directly satisfied by Kardecist Spiritist Centers, yet we have nothing like them. Elsie Dubugras shared her thoughts with me on how it is that a philosophy such as Kardec's Spiritism, that has been so successful in both healing and encouraging spiritual development, did not find a home in the USA and other "first-world" countries. She said, "The USA is too wealthy. In Brazil, we have a lot of poverty. The government moves very slowly and social welfare has been inadequate to address the needs of the people for food, medicine, child-care and education of the poor. We needed to find a way to take care of each other. Kardec's Spiritism provided the way."

In the following chapters we look more closely at the underpinnings of a Kardecist Center. My goal is to transmit how a Spiritist Center might take root outside of Brazil's cultural imprint. Brazil is changing at a rapid rate, as is the rest of the world. A Spiritist center is a living organism, and must adapt to and be appropriate in the way it nurtures the community where it is seeded. It seems there is fertile ground for Spiritism to grow in many places outside Brazil—anywhere people are looking for both a deepening understanding and practice of spiritual development, as well as effective forms of healing and addressing the needs of both rich and poor.

Chapter Two recounts the origin and history of these Centers. In Chapter Three we distinguish Spiritism from Spiritualism and religion. Chapter Four considers how Spiritist Centers support personal spiritual evolution. We'll look at the evolution of the human being, tied to reference points easily observable in a person's attitudes and actions. We consider how Spiritist centers are especially appropriate for people at specific stages of personal evolution. While, to some, Spiritism may seem obscure, invisible, meaningless or confusing, to others, thirsty for all that it offers, it appears as pure water in a beautiful oasis in the desert. Part Two takes you into the life experience of individuals who have participated frequently in activities of a Spiritist Center, and who have experienced profound healing. Most attended Spiritist centers revolving around more classical avenues of healing: energy passes, prayer, study of life principles according to Kardec, and training to be mediums and healers. One went to the unique Spiritist center that uses Paul Laussac's electromagnetic devices for healing.

It is important to recognize that Spiritist centers are evolving. A Spiritist center is not a static entity with a rigid external structure. It is acceptable for a Spiritist center to utilize new resources gathered from technology and from diverse cultures. If you choose to create a Spiritist center, you, too will make innovations as you adapt to your community's needs.

Part Three describes in more detail how a Center functions; especially the classes, preparation of teachers, and School for Mediumship, (so new to our culture). This is an attempt to help you determine what you may want if you are creating a Spiritist Center or using components to enrich a health care program that already exists. Chapter Eleven considers how to create a Center that is *right for your community*. Finally there are Notes, a Glossary, Suggested Reading list, and an Index.

Chapter Two

The History

How many people are involved? How did Kardecist Spiritism come about? Why have these Brazilian community centers retained their value for more than one hundred years? Why has their membership continued to increase? If they are so successful in healing, why don't we know more about them? Why are they so popular with the intelligentsia? What is happening in the present with Spiritism in Brazil?

Demographics

Although Kardecist Spiritism is also popular in the Phillipines,[1] there are more Kardecist Spiritists in Brazil than anywhere else in the world. Even though formal demographics record that eighty to ninety percent of Brazil is Catholic, an article in the Brazilian newsmagazine, Veja, ("Look," similar to Time Magazine in the USA) recently reported that 32 million Brazilians attend Spiritist activities[2]. This is close to twenty percent of the total population of 179 million. There are more than 6,500 Spiritist Centers throughout the country serving this population. In 2000, FEB (the Federation of Brazilian Spiritists) reported that 4.5 million Brazilians were listed as "members" of that organization.

Still, it is difficult to pinpoint exactly how many Brazilians utilize each Kardecist Spiritist Center. Since it was illegal to convene Spiritist activities during most of the 20th century, Spiritists learned to maintain anonymity and only keep a bare minimum of records.

In the 1980s the Brazilian government created a program for socialized medicine to provide basic medical care for the entire population. However, these programs were not adequate to take care of everyone's needs. People found it was typically a long wait to be seen by a physician, and rarely did one have the advantage of individualized care. To compensate for this lack, the rich preferred to go to private doctors and clinics; and both rich and poor continued to use diverse sources of healing, including complementary and alternative therapies. Although Spiritist Centers do not offer emergency medical care, the healing they provide is tailored to the individual's needs, and can be highly effective with chronic emotional and physical problems.

Enjoying both health and religious freedoms, Brazilians try to combine the best of what is available to them. While consulting doctors versed in the mainstream bio-chemical model of medicine, many go to mediums for healing and herbal remedies; while maintaining nominal membership in the Catholic Church, many choose to attend Spiritist classes and participate in Spiritist healing sessions.

Historical Perspective

There are several reasons why Brazil was fertile ground for seeding and nurturing Kardecist Spiritism. Brazil is a country that is more racially integrated than most. The population is built on inter-racial marriages among the Europeans who colonized Brazil, the indigenous Brazilian Indians, and the Africans who were brought to Brazil as slaves, centuries ago. Many of the people have at least some roots in the shamanic tradition. The phenomena of communication between disincarnate spirits and human beings, intrinsic to shamanic traditions, is more readily acceptable in such a culture.

Kardec's Spiritism dovetails in many other ways with the shamanic tradition: Both believe in the truth of reincarnation—that life is a process of perpetual evolution through many lifetimes, that everyone has sensitivities which go beyond the five physical senses, and that there is vast positive potential in spiritual healing. Similar to shamans (indigenous medicine men and women), Spiritists believe that we are in essence, eternal spirits having an experience of being in a body. Both shamans and Spiritists believe that it takes discipline and perseverance to be skilled in using psychic abilities; that developing these abilities, can contribute to healing from mental illness and being of service to one's community.

Another element in Brazilian culture that made it receptive to Kardec's ideas: Brazilians are a charitable, friendly, and community-oriented people. Many reach out to help those needy of medical help and social services, who are not being adequately provided for. Kardec recommends that charity be an essential aspect of spiritual evolution. This is very acceptable to Brazilians.

So, when Kardec's Spiritism came to Brazil in the late nineteenth century, it readily found a home there.

Hippolyte Rivail/Allan Kardec

How a Christian, French intellectual came to write seminal books on Spiritism is quite another story. It is a story worth telling, however, because it portends the willingness of intelligent, religious people to open to and value the unusual phenomena of communication with disincarnate spirits. The story of Kardec's Spiritism in Brazil illustrates how the belief in reincarnation, karma, spiritual evolution, and phenomena typically ascribed to parapsychology can fit within, and revitalize Christian life.

Hippolyte Rivail, (1804-1869), was devoted to improving public education, and helping common people to have more fulfilling lives. He was a well-respected professor who taught mathematics, astronomy, physiology, French, physics, chemistry, and comparative anatomy. He also authored popular books on spelling and grammar. He appealed to intellectuals; and, as a result, when his "Kardec" books came to Brazil, they were first widely read by intellectuals. Still today, middle and upper class intellectuals are the ones most often found in the advanced courses given at the Spiritist Centers, as well as volunteering their time as mediums and healers administering to those coming for healing.[3] Similarly, it is these well-educated intellectuals who follow the work of Spiritist leaders doing research in parapsychology, to find scientific evidence that the soul survives as spirit, after death.

"The time has come when the teachings of Christ can be interpreted in their fullest significance. The veil of allegory that He purposely used on many occasions must be lifted. Science must see beyond matter and acknowledge a spiritual perspective; religion must stop ignoring the fundamental laws of matter. Only in this way will both sides (science and religion) come together and learn to lean on each other. As a result religion will no longer be discredited by science. Its accordance with reason and with the compelling logic of the events of nature will give religion a new, unshakable power."
— A. Kardec.

When spirit communication began to be explored in France in the mid-1850s, Rivail visited several mediums to see for himself if there was any value in what they were doing. Rivail became intrigued with what he witnessed one night when "tables were circling around, jumping and even running, as it were, in such conditions that any doubts were dispelled. That was a fact: There must be a cause, I thought. Something very serious is behind all this stuff that serves merely to entertain the spectators." (May, 1855)[4] Rivail was watching what was then called, "spirit-rapping," a psychokinetic phenomena where a table would begin to move, by itself, without being pushed by any kind of physical force. Rivail concluded that the only explanation was that the table was being moved by energies in an invisible dimension, trying to make contact with human beings.

Rivail was told, through two mediums who were said to be channeling evolved spirits, that he had a great work ahead of him: to collate universal wisdom being channeled through numerous, independent mediums. Foreseeing the vast importance to science and religion of carefully investigating the phenomena, under the pen name of Allan Kardec, a name he believed to be from one of his prior lives, Rivail dedicated himself to this mission. During the last 20 years of his life he completed five books: In 1857: "*The Spirits' Book.*" It contains 1,018 questions he alleged to have posed to the spirits, and the answers he collected and collated from many mediums who had addressed various spirits with these same questions. It was the first significant book to propose the principles of Kardec's Spiritism, differentiating it from the more generic Spiritualism (see Chapter Three). In 1859: *"The Mediums' Book"* was printed. In 1864: *"The Gospel as Explained by Spiritist Doctrine."* In 1865: *"Heaven and Hell."* In 1868: *"Genesis."* After Rivail's death, *"Posthumous Works"* was published in 1890.

Some claimed that Spiritism was the knowledge of God's Spirit, a new revelation. Alvear, a Phillipine Spiritist, looked at the phenomena of Spiritism as "the first attempts of the Holy Spirit to communicate a new spirituality, a form of Christianity in which the Holy Spirit manifested itself through highly evolved Christian mediums."[5] Kardec suggested it fulfilled the word of God that said, "On the last day, my Spirit shall pervade all mankind, your sons and your daughters shall be the prophets, the young men shall see miracles, and the old women and men shall dream new dreams."

The Christian tradition does not apparently embrace the notion that the spirit world exists, that spirits are also evolving, and communication happens between the spirit world and the human world. Phenomena of this nature have been relegated to the twilight zone of ghost stories, or reserved for the esoteric, long-gone world of Jesus Christ, Moses and the Apostles, who were apparently unique in their ability to speak to God and/or Angels. From this perspective, people who say they can talk to God and/or the Angels are perceived as mentally ill or blasphemers. Direct communication with highly evolved spirits is not considered a potential of every human being.

Kardec's initial openness to explore mediumship, his willingness to discern the mediums who had something of value to share from those who were misguided, and his dedication to the work of presenting the best he found, has helped many people, of all faiths, make deeper commitments to realizing their potential for more intimate connection to spiritual dimensions. In Kardec's books they find principles that are practical, as well as doable. They find their way to forgiveness of themselves and others, increased joy, love, and peace.

In England, in 1936, the Archbishop of Canterbury, Cosmo Lang, investigated Spiritualism by commissioning a team of advisors for a span of three years. He wanted to know if Spiritualism was consistent with Christianity. He apparently was so embarrassed by the conclusions they presented, that he hid them from the public eye. They were lost until the 1970's, when they were finally published: Spiritualism, they reported, was not in opposition to Christianity and the evidence for the soul's survival at death was "most convincing."[6]

Kardec's Spiritism Comes to Brazil

According to David Hess, in his book, "*Samba in the Night*," Spiritism originally came to Brazil through homeopaths, who were already using magnetic healing and intuition as components of attending their patients. Hahneman, founder of Homeopathy, encouraged the use of magnetic healing as a means of increasing the effect of homeopathic remedies.

In the late nineteenth century, many homeopaths who had trained in Europe and then come to Brazil, were deeply dedicated to helping the poor. These doctors organized and founded the first private Spiritist group in Brazil shortly after 1848. In 1858, Kardec's "The Spirits'" arrived, igniting the zeal of these Spiritist communities. The first Kardecist Spiritist magazine, published in Brazil in 1869, was called "The Echo from Beyond the Grave." The first Spiritist group in Brazil to be incorporated (in 1873) was called "Group Confucius."

These first centers were not organized under any central authority. But, soon, there was a galvanizing event that made it necessary for a Brazilian Spiritist leader to step forward. In early 1890 an article in Brazil's new penal code banned all forms of Spiritism (Espiritismo). There were then, and still are, several forms of Spirit mediumship religions in Brazil. "Quimbanda" is one that uses "black magic" as a force for hurting enemies. "Macumba" is a disparaging term for any spirit mediumship religion with some African influence. "Candomble" is more of a pantheistic religion. Its rituals focus on paying homage to the "orixas," various deities having the power to confer favors. "Umbanda" emerged in early 20th century, mediating mainly with disincarnate beings who were black or indigenous Indians. (Kardecist mediums communicate more with incarnates who are white, of European descent, and intellectuals.) Every form of Spiritism was banned under the new code.

Responding to the threat of religious repression, Kardecist Spiritists began to rework the presentation of their philosophy, referring to it in terms of research in parapsychology. Intellectuals stepped forward as leaders of the movement. Even so, Spiritists were prosecuted legally up through the 1920s; their activities were still considered illegal in the 1930s and 1940s. Elsie Dubugras, a Spiritist leader, told me stories of how she and her friends had to sneak into meeting places in the dark of night in the 1940's and 1950's, hiding the fact they were meeting for Spiritist functions.

Bezerra de Menezes: a medical doctor and politician in the nineteen century is sometimes referred to as "the Brazilian Kardec." Just as Kardec codified Spiritism, Menezes unified it, bringing together various factions under the umbrella of a Federation of Brazilian Spiritists, "FEB." He remains a symbol of the ideal of Spiritist unity and self-discipline. His photograph is often placed in central areas of Spiritist Centers throughout Brazil.

The FEB was founded in 1884. Once Menezes took on its leadership in 1890, and continued for most of the 1890's, until his death in 1900, FEB became a central unifying force. Menezes two books, "Philosophical Studies," and "Insanity Through a New Prism," were instrumental in giving a scientific perspective to Kardec's Spiritist activities. This last book describes spirit obsession and its treatment. Menezes wrote that in cases of mental illness that show no sign of cerebral lesion, the cause is spiritual. That means that *spirit obsession* is a cause of profound mental illness and personal transformation may be a cure for most emotional problems (translated as "spiritual illness" during Menezes' time.) In articulating the effect the spirit world had on humans, Menezes mapped out a world of spirit-human interaction that was as real to most Brazilians as the world of repression and defense mechanisms was to the Europeans who were developing psychoanalysis at that time. Today, the FEB is still going strong.

Kardecist Spiritism gained in popularity when a humble Brazilian clerk, Chico Xavier, began to write popular books in the late 1930's. He was believed to be a channel for evolved spirits, in keeping with Kardec's writings. Like the American-born channel, Edgar Cayce, Xavier also gave direction for treatment to the ill who came to him for advice.

Xavier wrote more than three hundred and fifty books that clarify details, in narrative form, about where one goes at death, what it feels like to be "out of the body," and how a departed one can stay in communication with loved ones who are still "in body." They also illustrate that life continues to become happier as one grows spiritually. Andre Luiz, a physician and poet, and Emmanuel, a Jesuit theologian, are two of the most prolific entities Xavier is said to have channeled. These books were and are still very comforting and inspiring to those looking for answers to some of life's most important questions. They have made Kardec's teachings even more accessible to the general public.

Xavier was considered a living saint by Brazilians. During his life, the proceeds of the sale of all of his books were donated to charities throughout Brazil. Since millions of copies were sold, Xavier was able to be a sustaining support to many poor and underprivileged people. Brazilians appreciate the man's sincerity and generosity: despite the popularity of his books, Xavier continued to live a very simple life.

Another leader in the Kardecist movement was Edgard Armond (1894-1982). He had been a former commander in the Brazilian military before devoting himself to Spiritism. As a teacher and leader, he demanded a high degree of discipline from his students and the teachers and administrators of the FEESP, the Federation of Spiritists of San Paulo State. Armond was quite severe, and many were afraid of him; but, as a well-disciplined medium, he was also able to explain the components of mediumship to help others. The School for Mediumship at the FEESP was founded in 1946, during Armond's leadership there. It was said to be a cooperative effort between spirits who helped formulate what was needed, and Armond who brought it into being. In 1950, he published "Passes and Radiaçoes: Metodos Espiritas de Cura" ("Energetic Passes and Radiations: Spiritual Methods of Curing") which defines the practice and theory of healing by transmitting energy through laying-on of hands. This book, not yet translated into English, is still considered indispensable in classes at Spiritist Centers in Brazil that teach healing. The third edition was published in 1999. Armond's other book, "Mediumship," also not yet in English, is still in use as well. He was head of the "Fraternity of the Disciples of Jesus," which he founded in 1952, to acknowledge developed mediums who are dedicated to charity work. Armond passed away in 1982.

Hernani Guimaraes Andrade (1912-2002) was a parapsychologist considered to be one of the most respected scientists and intellectuals in Brazilian Spiritism, Before his death, Andrade published fifteen books and numerous papers on spiritual phenomena and paranormality. An engineer, mathematician and physicist, prior to becoming a parapsychologist, Andrade had taught at various universities in Brazil. After re-orienting his energies to study parapsychology in 1963, his base of operations was the Brazilian Research Institute of Psycho-Biophysics. He was known internationally for applying the same scientific rigor to his studies of parapsychology, that he had applied to his research in physics. He was a colleague of Ian Stevenson, a North American who researched and found significant evidence[7] of reincarnation. Andrade, in Brazil, thus provided a scientific anchoring to many of the underlying principles of Spiritism.

One exemplary leader who continues to teach at FEESP and other independent centers, is Martha Gallego Thomaz, born in 1915. She is one of the few remaining leaders who initially shaped Kardecist Spiritism in Brazil who is still alive. This diminutive woman, not five feet tall in heels, supervises five groups of five mediums simultaneously, while managing the flow of patients coming in for energy passes for physical healing at the Center. (Psychological and spiritual healing for de-possession and dis-obsession occurs in other rooms with developed healer-mediums.) Dona Martha welcomes the patient at the door with a hug and a kiss, then hold-ing the hand of the patient, leads him/her to a chair in the center of a circle of healers. As the patient settles him/herself, Dona Martha gives specific instructions to the mediums, e.g. "focus on the color green in the area of the heart to give it strength." She manages eighty to one hundred and fifty patients in one morning in this same way—all with loving sensitivity for each individual. Highly principled, she is firm with the mediums, wanting the best, while still maintaining her loving affectionate way. She, like Elsie Dubugras, is also a member of the Fraternity of the Disciples of Jesus.

Today's Leadership

Kardecist Spiritism is now at an important transition point. Its current leaders are passing on. Dona Elsie will be one hundred years old in 2004. Chico Xavier, the prolific writer who was considered a living saint in Brazil, died in 2001, at the age of ninety-four. What will happen to Spiritism as these great leaders pass into the spirit world is a timely question. I have asked several Brazilians to give me their feeling on the subject. No one has any certainty about the future.

After sixty years of contact with Spiritist leaders, often writing about them, or translating their work, Elsie was able to provide valuable perspec-tive. When asked, "Who are the leaders of Kardecist Spiritism today?" Elsie replied, " A good evolution is happening. People are not looking to leaders anymore, as much as taking authority for themselves. This means that Spiritism has truly entered people's homes. It is not just an activity limited to the Spiritist Centers. It is no longer dependent on special leaders."

Westerners just discovering Spiritism, worry that the structure of Kardecist Spiritism will dissolve before they can learn more from its most qualified teachers. Martin Mosquera, a translator volunteering at the Casa de Dom Inácio, the Center where John of God does his healing work, suggests, "We don't have to figure it out. We must only trust that God will show us the way. When it is time for something to happen, it will happen."

Not fully content with the vagueness of Martin's answer I thought, "We have some responsibility to initiate what we feel is right, not just wait for something to happen." In the *Gospel Explained by Spiritist Doctrine*, Kardec quotes a spirit who refers to Kardecist Spiritism:

"(These) ethical principles to live by will transform Earth into a planet that will become the home of a far greater number of evolved beings. This is the Law of Progress, to which all nature must submit. The Spiritist (principles) are a lever the Almighty makes use of to spring humanity toward a new era."

Although this was written in the 1860's, it indicates a direction for all humanity, ever more poignant today, as our world is more interconnected and cooperation is more important. It opens the possibility that Spiritism will be seeded in a way that contributes to progress, as this is the Law of Progress.

Are we are ready to bring Spiritist principles into our homes and communities, to improve our health care delivery systems, improve the effectiveness of community services for the poor, help those who are natural mediums to develop their skills, and hasten our progress toward effective health maintenance, brotherhood and spiritual enlightenment? This will indeed create a new era for mankind. We certainly don't have to call ourselves or our health care centers "Spiritist" in order to adapt Spiritist principles. They are free for the taking.

Brazilians are leading the way in their wise use of Spiritual healing, because of their way of putting Spiritism to action. They have a blueprint we can use both in their philosophy and in the way they put that philosophy into action. Perhaps Brazil may inspire the rest of the world toward its next steps in evolution. Some mediums I met believe this is true because our next level must be built upon a foundation of brotherhood, love and charity, qualities that Brazilian Spiritists have put in action for over one hundred years. We need only recognize that Brazil has developed something we are ready to learn about. Kardec's work, now 150 years old, is leading us in the direction of universal brotherhood, transcending the confines and habitual conflicts that spring from nationalism.

On a Personal Note: Problems with Translations

Questions I had while doing this research into Kardecist Spiritism: Why hadn't I ever learned about Kardec? He has such a wide following. Why have there been so few books (I found only two books for a general audience) written about the phenomena of Spiritism, a way of life so compelling to millions of Brazilians, and so effective in healing, developing psychic abilities and performing grassroots social welfare? I wondered, "Either I have fallen into uncharted territory or, the translations of Kardec's books have turned people away."

Answers: Kardec's books are referred to as his "doctrine." Most English dictionaries define "doctrine" as "creed" or "dogma that is advocated." Actually, Kardec's teachings offer 'principles to live by' – a much more palatable phrase to those looking for universal truth. He aligned himself and his writings with scientific rational principles regarding life. He asks that people read and think through what is suggested, not accepting anything as "truth" until it has been personally analyzed and deemed valuable. His books offer perspectives which stimulate creative and rational thinking, not dogmatism.

Another translation problem occurs over the use of the words, 'Gospel' and 'Evangelism.' Kardec asked the evolved spirits, with whom he said he was in contact, to comment on the teachings of the New Testament. "*The Gospel Explained by Spiritist Doctrine*" is the current English translation of one title, contains their answers. Readers can easily get the impression, because of the title, that it purports to put forth 'the gospel truth.' Actually, the title refers to a new interpretation of the Gospels of the New Testament, according to the principles set forth by the spirits consulted by Kardec.

Kardec's books have long gathered dust on the lowest shelves of many bookstores. Words like "Doctrine" and "Gospel" are not popular in the lexicon of progressive thinkers. Fundamentalists will probably not look to Brazil or a Frenchman for their Gospel.

If I hadn't traveled to Brazil and been so impressed by the Spiritism in action I saw there, I would also have overlooked Kardec completely. Even though in Brazil, a nation of almost 200 million people, reading Kardec is routine for those studying psychology, there was no mention of his work in my graduate school of psychology in the United States. That was my loss (and amazed the Brazilians I met who expected me, with a doctorate, to know all about Kardec.)

Finally, when I was able to get the books in the USA[8], I was delighted. Kardec's "Gospel" has opened my mind to new possibilities. "*The Gospel As Explained by Spiritist Doctrine*," in particular, impressed me as a book inspiring love in the highest sense, including a much needed ecumenical approach to religion. Kardec is inclusive, rather than exclusive. Kardec aspires to be based in contemporary science, rather than a doctrine that avoids scientific thinking. There is no mention of conversion. What is suggested is increasing awareness, discipline, service and study.

Chapter Three

Sorting Out Spiritism
vis a vis Spiritualism and Religion

"Christ, our Master, called himself Truth, not convention."

— Tertullian, noted Christian leader from Africa, (160-223AD)

As people in the West begin to examine Spiritism, one of their first questions is "What makes it different than Spiritualism, (a word we are more familiar with in the English language)? Are Spiritism and Spiritualism the same thing?" Secondly, they want to know, "Is Spiritism a religion?" These are important questions to answer for anyone considering founding a Kardecist Center or importing any of its components into our existing health care system.

Comparing Spiritism and Spiritualism

Spiritism and Spiritualism came into being at the same time—at the middle of the nineteenth century. In their beginnings, both Spiritism and Spiritualism referred to the belief in the existence of disincarnate spirits and the exploration of communication with them. As time went on, Spiritism and Spiritualism became quite different.

The first recorded spirit communication in the USA was in 1848. It was reported that Margaretta and Kate Fox, from Rochester, New York, were being bothered by the spirit of a disincarnate, who created psychokinetic phenomena (rattling furniture and dishes) around them to get their attention. According to the reports, this inexplicable activity only ceased when the sisters, evidently amused, devised a way to successfully communicate with the man beyond death, who claimed that his bones were buried in the basement of their house. He allegedly demanded that "You must proclaim this truth to the world," which resulted in their founding the first *Spiritualist* meeting in 1849, to facilitate more communication with spirits in a public venue. The story continues that fifty years later the bones, along with a peddler's box, were found in the place "he" described in the basement. This was long after the Fox sister's source of personal amusement had become an international sensation. Both the Spiritist and Spiritualist movements were born, and various kinds of "séances," groups that gathered to explore spirit communication, had spread to Europe, as well.

The great majority of Americans and Europeans viewed communicating with disincarnates as nothing more than a bizarre form of entertainment. But, by 1854, after phenomena was witnessed and verified by people believed to be credible individuals, the US Congress was petitioned to appoint a scientific commission to investigate paranormal phenomena. The investigation was met with skepticism and controversy. Numerous scandals had undermined the credibility of some of Spiritualism's foremost proponents. The Fox Sisters had succumbed to alcoholism, sensationalizing their activities, and seeking money. Thus, Spiritualism garnered a poor reputation, eroding efforts of scientifically minded people who wanted to explore the more serious side of psychic phenomena, i.e. how it could be applied to medicine, religion, and psychology.

From its very beginnings, Kardecist Spiritism was more philosophical and intellectual than Spiritualism. The philosophy of Kardec's Spiritism was built on the laws of cause and effect, and reincarnation. It asked people to study and come to terms with the Laws of God and Nature. Students were required to study, but not study to the point where the head dominates the heart. They believed that *study and good work done simultaneously creates a proper balance for spiritual development.* Brazilian Spiritists apply the philosophy they study to help others, including but not limited to assistance in healing. This is why Kardecist Spiritism has been referred to as a path of "practical Christian Spirituality[1]."

Spiritualism in the US and Europe lacks this solid intellectual, philosophical, action-oriented, and scientific basis. It also often lacks the charity work, and the directive for inner transformation—the action that is an expression of the philosophy. Followers of Spiritualism in Europe and the United States, believed in an indwelling spirit, and the fact that disincarnates can communicate and develop relationships with human beings and mediums. However, Kardecist Spiritists believe in reincarnation; whereas, not all Spiritualists do. It follows that many Spiritualists do not believe that the conditions of their present lives may be an effect of transgressions made in past lives. Spiritualists can become fascinated with the phenomena of communicating with Spirits, but entirely miss the important work of personal transformation, so essential to Spiritism.

From the *Gospel Explained by Spiritist Doctrine*:

"For some Spiritualist individuals, material ties are still too strong for them to let go of worldly things. A kind of mist surrounds their minds…They find it difficult to break away from their habits, and curb their appetites. They believe in the existence of spirit as a simple fact. Such belief, however, changes few or none of their inclinations. They see a small ray of light, but this isn't enough to guide them or instill aspirations that would allow them to overcome their tendencies. They get far more excited by spirit phenomena than the moral principles of the doctrine, which they find trivial and dull. All they are interested in, usually, is asking the spirits to reveal new secrets, never considering that they might not be worthy yet of penetrating God's mysteries. These…are the ones who've stood still by the wayside…because they were faced with the need for self-reform… Still, accepting some of the fundamental principles of the doctrine is the first step, and this will make it easier for them to take a second step in a future life."

Brazilian Spiritism also differs from Spiritualism in its organizational style and the way centers manage the financial aspects of maintaining themselves. It is not as bureaucratic as Spiritualism in the Northern

Hemisphere—particularly England. Spiritualists there have more clearly defined roles in their organization. They even have a ministry, which is not found in Brazilian Spiritism. European and North American Spiritualists also consider it perfectly acceptable to remunerate mediums for their work. Kardecist Spiritists believe one cannot be in communion with the most evolved sources of intelligence if one charges fees for spiritual work. They believe that the materialism implicit in charging money literally degrades one's connection to the potential purity of communicating with evolved spirits. Brazilian Spiritists, following Kardec, believe that where money is involved, one will only have access to less evolved spirits. A phrase often repeated in Brazilian Spiritist Centers: "That which is received for free (spiritual inspiration), should be freely given away."

Is Spiritism a Religion?

If Kardecist Spiritism is truly motivated by the highest spiritual inspiration, can we recognize Kardecist Spiritism as a religion that has been overlooked? Visiting a Spiritist Center one witnesses people doing things that are intrinsic to churches and synagogues: prayer, meditation, listening to inspired talks about the nature of life and death, discussing universal truths, organizing and doing charitable works, feeding the poor, attending to the sick. These people are oriented toward being of service.

Consider how we define religion:

The Oxford English Dictionary defines religion as "the recognition of superhuman controlling power, and especially of a personal God, entitled to obedience."

Webster's New World Dictionary defines religion as "1. belief in and worship of God or Gods. 2. a specific system of belief or worship, etc. built around God, a code of ethics, a philosophy of life, etc."

Random House Webster's College Dictionary's first definition of religion is: "a set of beliefs concerning the cause, nature, and purpose of the universe, especially when considered as the creation of a superhuman agency or agencies, usually involving devotional and ritual observances, and often containing a moral code for the conduct of human affairs."

Compendiums on religion can be vague and confusing. Both Huston Smith's "*The Religions of Man*," and "*The Oxford Dictionary of World*

Religions," (published in 1997 by Oxford University Press), self-described as " a wealth of unrivalled and unbiased authoritative detail," give no mention in their indices of "Spiritism." The Oxford Dictionary classified an African-Brazilian Spiritual group, Umbanda, in diverse ways, in just one paragraph as "a cult," a "religious complex," *and then* "a religion." It mentions people attending a "séance" and speaking with spirits, after which Kardec's name is referred to. This is ambiguous and misleading.

Aart Jurriaanse, a South African who compiled the channeled teachings of DK, "the Tibetan," defined religion as "man's relationships with the subjective worlds; it concerns his invocative approach to Deity for guidance and support with his daily problems, and the response evoked by these calls of distress." Religion is a process of invocation, response, and further dialogue. This experiential definition may lead one to think that Spiritist Centers are religious centers.

Ask a Brazilian if Kardecist Spiritism is a religion, and he/she will most likely answer. "No, It's a way of life."

Speak to Elsie Dubugras, and you get a different answer. Born in 1904, Dona Elsie ("Dona" is a term of respect for a woman) is an elder in the finest sense of that word—she is wise, and publicly recognized for her intellect, knowledge, and wisdom. Elsie has spent most of her life as a Spiritist. She is fluent in English, Portuguese and French. She has authored articles about parapsychology, Brazilian Spiritism, and metaphysics and is still a top editor and translator at a distinguished publishing house, Editora Tres.

Elsie does not hesitate, "Of course Kardec's Spiritism is a religion! Think of the Latin roots of the word religion. Re-ligio. It means to connect yourself again. *Spiritism connects you again to the experiences of the Divine that live within you.* Isn't that the essential motive of every religion?"

At the roots of every religion is the human longing to strengthen connection to what is sacred. It's a quest for meaning, purpose and value; described as a quest for contact with a universal mind.

Kardec's Spiritism has been effective in facilitating healing and connection to universal mind. It has been functioning for over a century, and yet remains marginalized and/or unrecognized. Perhaps we don't recognize it as a religion because of our prejudice against any "normal" person who claims to have communion with the sacred, and our hesitancy to challenge the authority of our priests and church rituals.

> "Spiritism is one of the purest religions on the face of the earth. It teaches people how to directly connect to God."
>
> —Elsie Dubugras

Kardecist Spiritism puts the experience of God and spirits back into the hands and hearts of each person. There are no rituals and no priesthood. In this way you are empowered to create your own connection. You get to cultivate your relationships with the spiritual realm, and be guided, as needed. You don't need a go-between with the Divine. Mediums mediate with sacred energy for healing but do not replace or detract from one's own personal connection. In fact, the mediums teach you how to strengthen your own connection to spiritual realms. Yet, this kind of education does not challenge the role of another religion, nor ask participants to make a choice between membership in a Spiritist Center and another religion.

Charity, caring for the well-being of others, is considered a key to one's own well-being and spiritual evolution. Kardecists are service oriented. They put their philosophy into action. Essentially this vitalizes a Christian principle: to watch out for our neighbors.

Brotherhood, extending oneself to others in the generous spirit of care and compassion, is considered essential practice for Spiritists. How one accomplishes this is unique to each person. The administrator directing one center I visited in San Paulo, Centro, told me that it took almost twenty years for her family to prepare themselves to start and manage the Center. They had to learn the lesson of being true brothers and sisters to each other: Caring for each other, and learning how to work as a coordinated team.

Kardecist Spiritism may or may not be a religion. Brazilians I spoke with don't seem to be concerned with resolving the question, one way or the other. More importantly, Spiritism is a way to bring the essence of all religion to life.

A Map of Spiritual Evolution

A graphic illustration in the meditation room at Busca Vida, a Spiritist Center in Brasilia, maps the way to spiritual evolution and differentiates it from a life motivated by materialistic gain. This graphic is one source of inspiration and education for patients wanting to achieve good health.

Diagrams copied with permission from Busca Vida, (see Chapter 6).

Spiritual Path

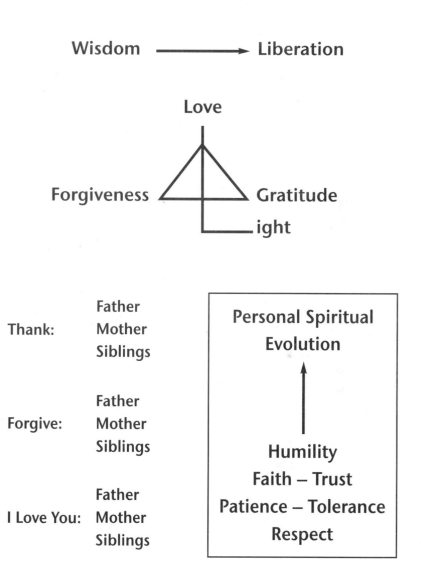

Wisdom ⟶ Liberation

Love

Forgiveness   Gratitude

ight

Thank:	Father Mother Siblings	**Personal Spiritual Evolution**
Forgive:	Father Mother Siblings	↑
I Love You:	Father Mother Siblings	**Humility Faith – Trust Patience – Tolerance Respect**

The Path of Spiritual Evolution leads to liberation and bliss. Wisdom gleaned on this path is built on a foundation of love, forgiveness and gratitude, all qualities attributed to spirituality. These qualities can only be created by forgiving, loving and being grateful to our parents, sisters and brothers. One who is evolving spiritually is developing more humility, faith, trust, patience, tolerance and respect.

On the other hand, ignorance leads to an attitude of fear that is often expressed in hateful attitudes. Ignorance is built on a foundation of selfishness and pride—attributes we ascribe to egotism. A person lost in the darkness of ignorance often complains, criticizes and judges others. These are all indicators of attitudes and behaviors of people who are not dedicated to a spiritual path of personal evolution.

Path of Materialism

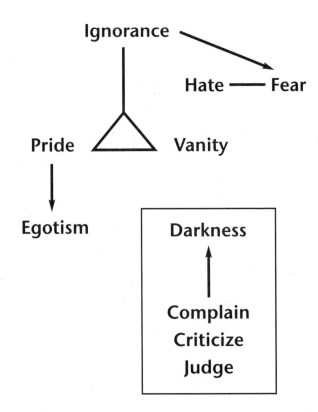

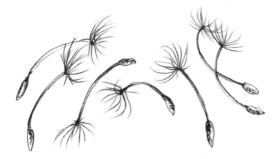

Chapter Four

Supporting Personal Spiritual Evolution

"Sown as an animal body, it is raised as a spiritual body."
— St. Paul in *I Corinthians, 15:44*

"Everyone starts at the same point; no one receives more from God than any other. The highest ranks are accessible to everyone. Getting there depends on the individual, who can choose to put forth the necessary effort and so reach the goal more quickly, or remain inactive for centuries and centuries in the quagmire of human matter."

—- *The Gospel Explained by Spiritist Doctrine*

This chapter gives a broad outline of personal spiritual evolution, and how we recognize it in ourselves and others. We reflect on how this evolution impacts our ability to heal from illness and maintain health. Spiritist Centers may or may not be religious centers, but do provide an avenue for one important aspect of religious life—inspiring personal spiritual evolution.

Levels of Spiritual Evolution

Following is a scale of spiritual development through five energy fields of consciousness, from the lowest, "The Physical level," up through the "Emotional," "Mental," "Integrated Personality Level," and finally, "The Level of Initiation." This conceptual framework was created by David Hawkins, MD, PhD., in "Power versus Force: An Anatomy of Consciousness," (1995). It is a reflection of what one finds in reading Aart Jurriaanse's "Bridges" (1978).

Hawkins is an American psychiatrist, researcher and author. He reported having a number of personal spiritual experiences that brought him extraordinary insight into the nature of consciousness, and strengthened his abilities to effect healing in his patients. After his personal breakthroughs, he became head of one of the most successful psychiatric clinics in New York City. Among other books, he co-authored "Orthomolecular Psychiatry" with Nobel Laureate, Dr. Linus Pauling.

Hawkins used "muscle-testing," aka kinesiology, to qualitatively define the levels of consciousness of people alive today.[1] Applied kinesiology began in the early 1970's when Dr. George Goodheart found that benign physical stimuli, e.g. a beneficial nutritional supplement, would increase the strength of certain indicator muscles, e.g. the deltoid muscle, and inimical stimuli, e.g. chemical sweetener, would cause those same muscles to weaken. John Diamond, MD. had found that subjects universally test weak when listening to deceits, and strong when hearing demonstrably true statements.

In 1975, Hawkins began exploring this same technique to distinguish truth and falsehood. Hawkins developed a scale of relative truth by which intellectual position, statements and ideologies could be rated on a scale from 1-1000. Over twenty years, 1975-1995, Hawkins analyzed and defined the full spectrum of levels of consciousness. From this he developed an anatomy of consciousness, a profile of the entire human condition, including the spiritual development of individuals and societies. He also observed that when a subject "went weak," this response was accompanied by a de-synchronization of the cerebral hemispheres.

Muscle-testing actually takes less than ten seconds to perform. What seems to be at work is the individual being tested taps into a "database of consciousness," a communally shared base of wisdom, belonging to all mankind. It is stored in a different "arena" of the mind than rational thought processes. This arena is non-local, impersonal and universal, but can be accessed through muscle-testing. Sound bizarre? Maybe, but before you close the book, consider that much of the work has been corroborated by worldwide research, in independent studies.

Jurriaanse, a South African, spent the last part of his life compiling the teachings of "DK," a disincarnate Tibetan Master, channeled by Alice Bailey, 1920-40s. One of Jurriaanse's books, *"Bridges,"* synthesizes the perennial wisdom from the Tibetan with other contemporary metaphysical works written in the final decades of the twentieth century. Jurriaanse's contribution was distilling more than twenty books of esoteric knowledge to make DK's teaching available to a general audience. The fact that Jurriaanse's perspective parallel's Hawkins, adds weight to the scale Hawkins developed.

The five levels described below appear to be sequential and defined within boundaries. However, as Hawkins writes, any classification of the levels of consciousness, like the one below, must necessarily be broad generalizations. As a person evolves he/she is predominantly engaged at one level, and, from time to time has experiences of other levels, thus *the boundaries of each level are permeable.* For example, the highly evolved healer may experience a craving for a certain kind of food, or difficulty in completely forgiving a certain person for some hurtful circumstance. Satisfying the craving for food is in keeping with the Physical level; holding on to resentment, or desire for revenge, is characteristic of the Emotional Level. Similarly, a person on the Mental Level may have one or more extraordinary, inspiring spiritual experiences portending future levels of growth. Hawkins says, in some instances, *the levels may overlap or even appear to develop simultaneously.*

Both Hawkins and Jurriaanse agree, the process of evolution varies from soul to soul depending on one's own volition. It varies in rate of growth, and the characteristics of growth.

Further complicating our ability to make simple distinctions, says Hawkins, is that levels of consciousness in any one person are always mixed, i.e. a person operates on one level of consciousness in one domain of life, and on another level of consciousness in another. We can only determine an individual's overall level of consciousness by the sum total effect of all the levels on which he/she operates. Even though, a clearly defined sequence of evolution is artificial, Hawkins suggests one reference point to determine the level of consciousness: *the principles to which a person is most committed.*

Realize, too, that the progressive steps described below are said to cover innumerable incarnations, spread over millions of years. Hawkins writes that during the early stages of development, when the soul has not yet infused the personality and emotional ups and downs characterize life, man's evolution is slow. Toward the later stages of development, the pace picks up, and evolution in the last stages can be very fast.

The Physical Level

According to Jurriaanse, approximately fifteen million years ago human consciousness began developing in humanoid physical forms. Throughout the next nine million years we began to develop self-awareness. This brought an ability to consciously observe our physical body's animalistic tendencies (fighting for food, or the best area of land, or a sexual partner), as well as expressions of some complex feelings (jealousy, lust, frustration, etc.). Like the rest of the animal kingdom, the motivation was instinctive, and the purpose was survival; but now we could observe ourselves while we were engaged in our lives.

Although people who are on the Physical level of consciousness can acknowledge the existence of more powerful forces in the world, there is, as yet, as Jurriaanse puts it, little motivation to develop higher states of consciousness.

People on the Physical level of consciousness, says Hawkins, are characterized by emotional states associated with feeling as if they are powerless victims. Humiliation, blame, despair, regret, anxiety, craving, hate, and scorn are typical. These emotional states are a reaction to experiencing life through belief systems that increase feelings of shame, guilt, apathy, grief, fear, desire, anger and pride. All of these reactive emotional states render both the individual and the society unable to act in ways that create loving community.

Physiologically, the reactive emotional states cause a release of adrenaline. When a person is continually immersed in emotional states and negative attitudes causing adrenaline release, the inevitable result is an erosion of physical, emotional and/or mental health. The "emergency emotions" suppress the immune response, causing both weakness and enervation of specific organs, dependent on the stressor.

My guess is rarely would such a person primarily on this level of consciousness be attracted to Spiritism. Why? Spiritism is not consistent with the belief that we are powerless victims, rather it is based on the belief that we are powerful co-creators who have the potential for highly evolved states of consciousness. Also, an individual at the Physical level is not yet engaged with his/her own resources of self-knowledge and intuition, and therefore often chooses to place authority for spiritual well-being into the hands of an authority figure, e.g. a priest representing the authority of the Church. Similarly, he/she is likely to put total faith in a licensed physician, rather than empower his/her own resources for self-healing in conjunction with a reasoned scientific approach to health care. Hawkins suggests that even now, the Physical level of consciousness manifests as "a habit" of putting one's faith in authority, rather than thinking, taking responsibility, and assuming authority for some of one's own life choices:

"The current elevation of science to the status of infallible oracle is an expression of our insecure compulsion to feel there is some kind of a measurable, universally predictable objective world 'out there' upon which we can rely."

Religious life, for those on Physical levels, is perceived as a set of relationships (with God and the Saints, as well as the priesthood of the church) to be managed so one will not be too harshly victimized by an all powerful judge. If not negotiated properly, there is the risk one may land in Hell, for Eternity.

The Emotional Level

Whereas a person is motivated in an instinctual way on the Physical level, an individual's desires are more connected to one's personality on the Emotional Level. Hawkins writes that motivation, on this level, is *both* instinctual, and designed to satisfy personal emotional needs. The beginnings of the aptitude for love start at this level, but it is typical that loving feelings are tainted by self-serving desire. The capacity for devotion exists, but is often accompanied by unreasonable, negative feelings, i.e. feelings of devotion to some who are more intelligent and wise exist alongside hatred toward others. Inner conflict, turmoil and ambivalence are common at the emotional level of consciousness.

Hawkins asserts that the behavior of eighty-five percent of the human race is currently determined by a mixture of the physical and emotional levels of consciousness. (In later work, he suggests that this percentage is beginning to decline, because people are evolving.[2]) People on the Emotional level experience waves of strong emotion in reaction to what they experience. To the extent that they are unable to avoid this reactivity, they feel victim to their own emotional states.

On the Emotional Level, the purpose of religion is to create positive feelings between the Source, or God, and oneself. This satisfies a desire for security, a sense that some things are predictable and can be depended upon. Again, there is the need to negotiate with a power who will both judge you either worthy of heaven or hell, and determine where you belong at the end of your life on earth.

Hawkins determined that repetition of waves of emotion in both physical and emotional levels of consciousness weaken the system, creating fertile ground for illness of all kinds to take hold.

According to Hawkins, when a person becomes able to make choices about where to place his/her attention, it becomes possible to stop being immersed in negative feelings by choosing a positive focus. When the person can apply his/her will to consistently affirm the positive, and face the unknown with a willingness to learn from every experience, then he/she can transition to the more evolved levels.

However, Hawkins generalizes, after reaching this kind of inner maturity, all levels are positive, empowering both the individual and his/her community to live more harmonious, peaceful lives. These individuals become readily interested in communities offering resources for spiritual development, like Kardecist Spiritist centers.

The Mental Level

According to Hawkins (1995), only 14.96% of human beings are now progressing upwards through the Mental and/or Integrated Personality levels of consciousness.

At the Mental level the emotional body becomes increasingly more refined. Rather than looking to material things to find emotional satisfaction, a person has higher aspirations for intellectual understanding. Further maturity on this level means that emotional satisfaction comes from nurturing these higher aspirations. Subsequently when the intellect, as such, no longer satisfies the inner urge towards self-improvement and deeper understanding, a person tends to look for increasing awareness of subjective realms. The inner life becomes fascinating. This person can see and understand the concept that there are Natural Laws in life, e.g. the law that all actions have consequences, and all effects have causes (Karma). He/she is also becoming conscious of the Soul. Through increasing focus on the Soul, the personality becomes "soul-infused," absorbing qualities associated with the Soul. New emotional capacities become accessible e.g. forgiveness, optimism, and trust. One's personal values also become more distinct, and more capable of honoring others. Altruism, wisdom, idealism, group service, sound discernment, understanding, sacrifice, perseverance, compassion, steadfast love and good will are qualities that grow as the personality becomes more Soul-infused. It is at this level that the mind becomes able to use the capacities of the physical brain as a tool.

On the Mental level, when there is a dawning of real connection to the Soul, religion can become a facilitator, enhancing that sacred connection, even evoking that connection. Here begins the breakdown of the notion that God is only outside of each person, as Divinity is now felt and experienced as having a place inside of each person.

Whereas the joy of developing the intellect first comes forward, the Mind, a manifestation of the Soul, eventually predominates as the source of intelligence. Like the conductor of a symphony, it begins to regulate the body, brain and emotions to further positive values and focus on positive emotions.

"IQ is merely a measure of academic capacity for logically comprehending symbols and words. The values that one lives by are more definitive of genius than IQ...Genius can be more accurately identified by perseverance, courage, concentration, enormous drive and absolute integrity. Talent alone is not enough. Dedication of an unusual degree is required to achieve mastery, and in the simplest definition, one could say that genius is the capacity for an extraordinary degree of mastery in one's calling."
— David Hawkins, MD

Consciousness can still descend temporarily to lower levels, as no one is capable of being in these highest levels all the time. However, each person must remain vigilant over his/her own consciousness, and continue to use will forces to determine that actions and thoughts are positive.

Within the Mental Level and on to Levels of Integrated Personality, pain and illness are no longer perceived as a judgment or punishment from God, but a "wake-up call." What does this mean? Illness may require that we stop our ordinary activities for a period of time, reflect on what caused the problem, rectify the stresses that led to the problem, and thus stop feeding the source that nurtures the problem. If used in this way illness can give us time to reconnect with our intuition and inner source of guidance. It can give us time to re-evaluate our priorities: "Am I doing what is most important for me to do? Have I gotten too caught up in what others expect of me? Am I too immersed in the hustle and bustle of life?" With a potentially terminal illness, we examine our mortality, and are more open to experience both what is mortal and that which is immortal.

The Integrated Personality Level

According to Hawkins, it is at this stage that, body, emotions and intelligence are under the control of the Mind, to be used for specific purpose, as directed by the will. The personality becomes increasingly more integrated, as body, emotions and intelligence become capable of working together as a unit. Wisdom, or knowledge with understanding, becomes more evident at this stage.

The person is consciously deciding to focus on becoming centered in the Soul. Focus extends outward to the world in reverence and compassion for all forms of life. The happiness of others becomes a motivating force.

What Spiritists consider intrinsic to healing—personal transformation, "reforma intima"— is essential to this level of development. A person at this level understands that study, meditation and service to one's fellow man are the most effective tools for accomplishing personal transformation. Being part of a Spiritist Community gracefully dovetails with this understanding.

As a person gives him/herself to a path of devotion to the well-being of the human family, he/she becomes increasingly more serene.

The notion that religion can be used to facilitate spiritual evolution, the progress toward increasing sense of Oneness with God, becomes increasingly more real as a person evolves past the Mental level into Integrated Personality and beyond.

Levels of Initiation

Jurriaanse recognized that as an individual increases his/her connection to the soul, and its energetic vibration, his/her personal "mission" (unique contribution to evolution) becomes revealed. The light of intuition is no longer obscured by the rational mind, so one senses one's mission more clearly. Now an individual becomes free to dedicate him/herself to his/her unique path without feeling constrained by the limits of personality and obsolete thinking patterns. There is a wondrous feeling of liberation, and, at the same time, empowerment in the pursuit of one's mission. Overarching the uniqueness of one's path is a profound connection to all life. Deepening that connection, takes one into new levels of initiation[3].

Spiritists, as well as DK, use the word "perfection" to describe the ultimate goal of spiritual evolution. *The motivation to achieve this level is not self-improvement; the purpose is to become a better instrument, or channel, for the highly evolved spirits to use in the service of creating a more highly evolved world. The closer one is to the ultimate ideal of spiritual union with the Divine, the more one can be of service to his fellow man.* The individual at this level knows that making a contribution accelerates spiritual evolution for all beings. Thus, his/her motivation for personal enlightenment becomes increasingly more immersed in empowering the evolution of the whole human community. Ultimately, the enlightenment of all of humanity is the only goal.

Hawkins (1995) finds that only 0.04 percent of the human race are currently in the "Initiatory" levels. Mediums and healers who are dedicated volunteers at Spiritist Centers are deliberately developing Integrated Personality and Initiatory Levels. Therefore, people who want to move into these higher levels would find support for that endeavor by taking part in mediums training and other activities at a Kardecist Center.

Subjectively, there is increasingly closer alignment with one's "Higher Self " (inner Divinity). One develops the habit of listening to, then following the direction of the Higher Self, rather than the more self-centered dictates of the personality. Paralleling the development of attending the Higher Self is an increase in the ability to perceive the spiritual worlds: hear and/or see disincarnates, perceive the way subtle energy radiates from a patient's body and vitalizes the systems of the body.

States of serenity and bliss are characteristic of this level of growth, as is wisdom. The emotional states associated with the personality are replaced by states of being which radiate out to others. These states of being are joy, peace, and enlightenment.

> "The key to joy is the unconditional kindness to all life,
> including one's own, that we refer to as compassion."
> — B.J. Eadie in *"Embraced by the Light"*

According to Hawkins, in the most advanced initiatory levels of consciousness, the individual has re-oriented his/her life so that the subjective world is more significant than the objective world. Time and activities are devoted to spiritual goals. Prayer, meditation, and healing work, where one is in communion with highly evolved, intelligent sources, become the optimal avenues for contributing to the evolution of mankind. The Christ, and all the Masters who have formerly developed the highest levels of consciousness, become available through telepathic contact. One no longer needs a medium, priest, or any kind of mediator to commune directly with the sacred.

> "The inherent sense of Divinity present in every human
> heart, must ultimately lead each individual soul to synthesis with the ONE."
> — Aart Jurriaanse

This level is consonant with the new theoretical physics. David Bohm writes, "Everything in the universe is connected with everything else." When one experiences this connection, one realizes it is a human potential, everyone can experience it. One also realizes the enormous responsibility one has:

"We shall eventually have to accept responsibility for every thought, word and deed we beget and re-experience exactly whatever suffering we have caused...Every act, thought and choice adds to a permanent mosaic; our decisions ripple through the universe of consciousness to affect the lives of all...Even if one sits isolated in a cave, his thoughts influence others whether he wishes it or not. Every act or decision you make that supports life supports all life, including your own. The ripples we create return to us. This, which may once have seemed a metaphysical statement, is now established as a scientific fact.

Everything in the universe constantly gives off an energy pattern of a specific frequency which remains for all time and can be read by those who know how. Every word, deed and intention creates a permanent record. Every thought is known and recorded forever. There are no secrets; nothing is hidden, nor can it be. Our spirits stand naked in time for all to see. Everyone's life, finally, is accountable to the universe."

— David Hawkins, MD

Any experience of this Oneness, although exhilarating and awe-inspiring, has a profoundly transformative and sobering effect. When we perceive the Oneness, our Souls must also be willing to assume responsibility for our part in the drama. We no longer can rest in the luxury of ascribing ultimate spiritual authority to the church or any priest. It is up to each one of us, as individuals, to manage our thoughts and our behavior. We are influencing everything all the time. It is up to us whether that influence is positive or negative. Do we radiate more positivity or negativity into the system of all of life? We have become simultaneously very powerful and very humble in the face of the Source of which we are part.

The motivations and states of being associated with the Levels of Initiation enhance the optimal functioning of the body, writes Hawkins. The body releasing more endorphins that have a tonic effect on all the organs is but one manifestation of this phenomena.

"Generally speaking, physical and mental health are attendant upon positive attitudes...It is generally held by traditional medicine that stress is the cause of many human disorders and illnesses. The problem with this diagnosis is that it does not accurately address the source of the stress. It looks to blame external circumstances, without realizing that *all stress is internally generated by one's attitudes*. It is not life's events, but one's reaction to them that activates the symptoms of stress. A divorce can bring agony or relief. Challenges on the job can result in stimulation or anxiety, depending on whether one's supervisor is seen as a teacher or an ogre."

— David Hawkins

This is another reason we find Spiritist Centers to be effective places for healing. It is not only receiving energy passes that promotes good health; the further one progresses in spiritual evolution, the easier it is for one's body to maintain good health.

Faculties of the Spiritual Man or Woman

Having outlined the evolution of humankind, it is useful to summarize the capacities of a person who is working at the highest levels. This is not to enumerate "powers," or illustrate how powerful a person is who has achieved this level, nor to encourage the development of power for selfish, egotistic purposes, but rather, to acknowledge what that person is capable of doing in service of the evolution of humankind. In fact, when a person has reached these high levels, Jurriaanse writes, "the need to inflate the ego automatically falls away."

The man or woman at this level has *developed extra-sensory perceptions and paranormal abilities*. He/She is able to consciously receive and transmit telepathic communications from peers, as well as from disincarnates. He/She has deliberately developed communications with highly evolved spirits who offer spiritual guidance. He/She is also in the habit of obeying promptings coming from the Higher or Divine Self.

Along with this refined telepathy, comes a finely tuned intuition, and the desire and will to obey the intuition. This is employed to discern truth from falsehood, without relying on objective determinants or moralizing. "Whether it is wrong to kill other human beings may be a moral dilemma at lower levels of consciousness; at higher levels the very question is ridiculous. Conventional morality is, therefore, only a provisional substitute for a faculty of higher consciousness," writes Hawkins. There is also the capacity to articulate into words what is recognized as truth. One might use this capacity in medical intuition: to perceive what is making the body ill, and translate that subtle perception into words to help the patient and his/her doctor create a diagnosis and treatment protocol.

The capacity to be a healing force comes naturally to a person who has developed into the higher levels. In the process of growth, he/she has come to understand vital forces and energies. He/She understands how to manipulate them to relieve both mental and physical suffering in other people.

Unless a person has developed the habit of consistent moral behavior, having the above capacities is only evidence of unusual potentials. What Spiritism stresses over and over again is that the spiritual person has *established a way of being in the world that is motivated by compassion and goodwill.* "Right Action," doing what is beneficial for the largest number of people as often as possible, comes naturally. This is not the way of martyrdom, and inflicting undue pain on oneself; rather a path of service, that brings profound joy.

> "The person who has arrived at a habitual state of unconditional Love will experience anything less as unacceptable. As one advances in the evolution of his individual consciousness, the process becomes self-perpetuating and self-correcting, so that self-improvement becomes a way of life."
>
> — David Hawkins, MD

New Groups/New Religions

As more people evolve into the Mental level and Levels of Initiation, we will need new forms of spiritual groups that can keep up with the conscious evolution of humanity. We need groups dedicated to facilitating spiritual evolution, who accommodate our new intellectual understanding of levels of consciousness, and also appreciate and assimilate scientific breakthroughs that give a foundation to higher levels of consciousness. We need a way of facilitating personal evolution that allows for billions of pathways to "salvation," the return to Oneness, not just one religion, claiming the favored path. Even though we can define levels where a person has particular motivations and satisfactions, there are as many pathways to those higher levels as there are people.

As Jurriaanse writes, DK suggests that these new groups, (he referred to them as "new religions"), will be based in the practice of invocation and evocation. He suggests they will gather to invoke the presence of highly evolved spirits, who share with the group their energy and their wisdom. This will have a profoundly beneficial affect on both the individuals as well as the community, as we will enhance our cooperation with those most able to stimulate higher forms of evolution.

It seems that the Spiritist Centers are a model for the kind of new group that DK spoke about. At Busca Vida, I was invited to participate in several prayer/meditation meetings that began by invoking Masters from the Spiritual realms, receiving communication from these Masters, then sharing the communications together for mutual inspiration. Both the contemporary Spiritist centers and the more traditional Spiritist Centers gather to evoke more highly evolved beings.

"...Future religion will accentuate the invocative approach from man to Divinity, and the response which will consequently be evoked. Greater attention will therefore in future be given to the art of Science of Invocation and the powers which will thereby be evoked.

The vast possibilities of Group Work and the increased power which can be generated by concerted invocative activities, will be emphasized. This will lead to the observance of worldwide sacred festivals, when humanity as a whole will direct its united petition to God, thus inevitably evoking far more potent results.

...Attainment of this ultimate goal can no longer be prevented by any adverse powers, but the rapidity of accomplishing these ideals will depend on the consecration and persistence with which man is going to apply himself to this most demanding task."

— Aart Jurriaanse, referring to the wisdom of DK

PART TWO

Portraits of Contemporary Centers

Four different kinds of centers are described in this section through the stories of people who have experienced healing there. One center is in a small country town in the high planes of central Brazil, another in the suburbs of Brasilia, and two are in downtown San Paulo. Each Center has its own signature, all are united by shared values and principles, and yet each has developed its own organizational structures. Hopefully this will give you ideas about how you can take one or more components of Spiritist Centers and blend them into a community health center in your own town, or, create your own new Spiritist Center.

Chapter Five

Palmelo

O amor nao exige
O amor nao recrimina
O amor e doacao que nao se cansa
    E compreensao que nao se nega.

Love doesn't make demands
Love doesn't recriminate or judge
Love is a gift that never ends
Love is comprehensive understanding
    Without negativity.
                  — Joaninha Darque

Joaninha Darque was a terribly ill, crippled girl of eleven when she came to Palmelo, Brazil, in 1959. She was also highly sensitive and intelligent—a young medium in her own right, who had most likely developed extrasensory perception in previous lifetimes. In 1959, she predicted her own death within a few hours.

During her last stay in Palmelo, before she passed away, Joaninha became close friends with Bartolo Damo. Damo believes, that since her death, Joaninha's spirit has remained closely connected to Damo and his unique work at the Spiritist Center of Light and Truth.

Damo is the head of this center at Palmelo, its most well respected medium and teacher of other mediums. On Sunday mornings, when he acts as the community's medical intuitive, and feels that Joaninha is often there, one of the spirits who whispers in his ear, giving him information about the patient in front of him seeking diagnosis and treatment. Damo recognizes her presence when he feels pressure around his little finger, as if it is being held by the hand of a young girl. Then, he listens carefully, and speaks out loud to the patient standing in front of him, transmitting in his own voice what has been recommended by this invisible spirit, who continues to serve humanity even out of the body, as a dis-incarnate.

Palmelo, a small town of three thousand people in the center of Brazil, is 70% Spiritist. Although several Spiritist centers serve the town, the Center of Light and Truth is the town's only Kardecist center originally founded by Jeronimo Candinho in 1929, following the advice of Euripedes Barsanulfo, a great Spiritist leader. In 1953, Palmelo founded a free-standing psychiatric hospital named after Barsanulfo. Since that time, the hospital and community has had an excellent reputation for helping people who are psychologically disturbed. Following is a list of resources at this Center:

- Euripedes Barsanulfo Hospital (psychiatric).
- Consultation with a medical intuitive.
- Psychic surgery by various mediums.
- Private consultations with the head of the Center.
- Automatic writing sessions.
- Dis-obsessions open to the public once a week.
- Basic Classes in the philosophy of Kardec.
- Training for Mediums and Healers and those learning Automatic writing.
- Inns that specifically cater to visitors coming for healing.
- A home for abandoned elders.
- A day care center for young children.

In 1997 UNESCO, the United Nations Educational, Scientific and Cultural Organization, recognized this Center as an historical asset serving all humanity. Palmelo is, in fact, the only city in the world founded by Kardecist Spiritists as a center for their activities and charitable works.

Damo is not a physician, nor is he Brazilian. In fact, he came to Brazil from Italy in 1949, at the age of 23. Ten years later, he came to Palmelo, and was "put to work" immediately by the administration of the Center, because his gifts as a medium were so strong. Damo described to me, that as a young boy, he had seen spirits. They were as real to him as spirits incarnate in bodies. He describes reaching out to them to hug them, as a child would affectionately greet a playmate. Of course, his parents were afraid their son was insane, and consulted a psychiatrist. Fortunately for Damo, the chosen doctor knew that psychic abilities were not a sign of mental illness, but a potential gift. Even so, Damo fainted when he over-heard the doctor telling his father, "Your son sees spirits." At the tender age of 10, Damo knew this meant he was out of the ordinary. He didn't want to be so different from the other 'normal' children.

By young adulthood, Damo had retained his gifts, but had not had the training necessary to use them in the best possible way to serve others. Being "put to work" under the guidance of a supervisor was part of his training, as well as recognition of his abilities. He also needed to work, to help him become more balanced, as at that time in his life he was emotion-ally unstable. It's not an easy thing to be born into a world where most people think you are insane, even you yourself wonder if it may be true, if you communicate with spirits.

Of course, the Brazilian authorities keep an eye on Damo. Like para-professionals in the USA, he does not have the licensed authority to diag-nose, nor give treatment for illnesses. The police have attempted to arrest him for practicing medicine without a license. In fact, Damo is sharing his insight with people about their physical and psychological problems by looking at their subtle energy bodies. Damo also suggests to some people that they stay in Palmelo and have psychic surgery. Legal authorities wonder, "Isn't that a form of treatment?"

"But," says Damo with a broad smile, "How can they do that? I don't touch anyone. I don't do physical surgery. I don't charge anyone for my services. And, I don't prescribe any medications. If I sense a patient needs prescription drugs, or medical treatment, I send them to a physician."

When I first visited Damo, in March, 2003, he recounted the story of a Lt. Colonel of the police, (who happened to have high blood pressure), and was sent to check on Damo, and possibly arrest him for performing the services of a physician. Damo's way of doctoring gave the policeman no evidence of illegal behavior. However, while he was sitting in Damo's office he began to have a stroke. Damo explained to me that he focused his spiritual strength on the man from across the room. The policeman not only returned to normal at that time, but since the time he was in Damo's intensified energy field his blood pressure has returned to (and remained) normal. Something was arrested that day, but it wasn't Damo.

Medical Intuition

When he is working as a medical intuitive, Damo sits flanked by female mediums on his left and male mediums to his right. These assistants remain quietly meditating and/or praying, in a state of mind in which they are supportive of Damo's psychic work. By being focused in higher states of consciousness as they sit near Damo, they act like a battery, charging an engine. Damo, after a prayer setting his intention to be of service, uses his "clairaudience," his ability to hear the advices being dictated to him by spirits of higher intelligence who want to help. He also uses his own intuition, and "clairvoyance" (a kind of x-ray vision which allows one to see into the state of mind, body and spirit of the patient).

One Sunday morning in October, 2003, the second time I experienced Damo as a medical intuitive, I entered the hall of the Center, where I gave my name to a receptionist. After everyone had entered, (about fifty visitors), the doors were closed. Our names were then called out and we sat waiting our turn in line. Then, in front of the watching bank of mediums, and the other waiting visitors, Damo gave each visitor a "reading," outloud, relating what he saw clairvoyantly and heard clairaudiently. One person at a time stood about eight feet in front of him. Three mediums (one to the right, one to the left, and one behind) each used both their hands doing energy passes, sweeping motions in the air, about five inches from my body, from above my head to the area of my upper legs. When I experienced this, I felt as if veils were being cleared away to make it easier for Damo to see into me. I also felt the energy passes as calming and strengthening. I felt very cared for.

Damo then called out, "It would be good if you came here for psychic surgery on your eyes. If you can't stay here for the required week of surgery and convalescence, it will be okay. But, have your eyes checked. You also have tension in your head. Cut back on eating sugars and salt.

Be sure to wear sunglasses to protect your eyes." He was right. This was the only health issue I had.

An assistant seated behind me took notes, handing them to me when I left. On it was also printed "this exam is valid for thirty days." It listed the inns authorized to host psychic surgeries and care for patients during convalescence. It invited me to come to Damo's office if I had any doubts or questions. On the bottom of the note was printed in big block letters: "All that we suffer is a result of the seeds of hurt and injury we have sown." The Center was using this paper as another opportunity to reflect on karmic action, suggesting that every action one does, every thought one has, either results in more love or more negativity. Consistently, visitors to Palmelo and other centers are reflecting on their responsibility to choose negativity or positivity. One is reminded, if you choose negativity, it may eventually lead to illness; if you choose positivity, it leads to better health and spiritual growth.

Dis-obsession and De-Possession

On two occasions I was invited by Damo to watch the dis-obsession in the assembly room at the mental hospital. Again, Damo was the central figure, flanked by twenty seated mediums, sitting quietly beside him in a room marked off from the assembly hall by a four foot high dividing wall. After the patients were in the hall, men on one side, women on the other, one of the mediums read an inspiring passage out of one of Kardec's books, then led the group in a recitation of the Lord's Prayer. Subsequently, mediums attended each of the patients, individually, providing energy passes. These standing mediums spent only a few minutes on each patient, silently sending energy to liberate them from obsession or possessing entitites. Meanwhile, the seated mediums held hands, often shaking or grimacing as the presence of negative disincarnates was acknowledged and released. After each patient was attended to, the Lord's prayer was repeated out loud by everyone. The patients were then ushered out of the assembly room, returning to the adjacent hospital, and the mediums exited from the main door, onto the street.

Marcel's Schizophrenia

I heard many stories of successful healings, under the guidance of Damo, from people who come to visit the Center at Palmelo. One of the most fascinating and impressive is the story of Marcel:

Marcel Teles Marcondes came to Palmelo in the Spring of 2002. Although he had enjoyed a normal life with satisfying work as a travel agent, and many friends, he began to experience emotional problems when he was in his late 20's (in 1996). His father, Arnold Marcondes Filho, a bank manager for the Bank of San Paulo State, Banesba, was able to afford excellent medical care for his son, and took Marcel to the best psychiatrists in San Paulo.

Marcel was first diagnosed with depression, then schizophrenia. Anti-psychotics were prescribed as well as sleep medication. The prognosis: Marcel would have to manage his symptoms with these strong medications for the rest of his life. But the medications never made him feel well. When he was committed to a psychiatric clinic for twenty days, the hospital environment only added to his stress. His parents then tried touring Brazil with Marcel for eight months in a motor home, to help him relax. Marcel continued to experience bizarre delusions: seeing and feeling crabs and spiders crawling all over him, grabbing at him. He could turn unpredictably aggressive and hostile for periods of time. Sometimes, he would hear two to three voices in his head talking to him, simultaneously.

Although the family was Catholic and had been advised by their physicians not to trust the services of Spiritist healers, they took a chance and drove Marcel to Palmelo. He was committed to Euripedes Barsanulfo Hospital and stayed there for one hundred days.

As an in-patient, Marcel continued on his medication, under the care of a licensed psychiatrist. Marcel also participated in the mainstream modes of therapy: physical activity (playing soccer or gardening), doing occupational therapy, and attending group therapy three times a week. He also participated in the Spiritist activities. "Dis-obsession" and "de-possession" were performed to rid him of negatively motivated disincarnates who had attached themselves to his energy field. This was not an exorcism as we know it, as there were no special rituals or incantations performed by a priest. There were only "energy passes" performed by healer/mediums, who transmitted healing energy to Marcel, without touching him. Three times a week he and the rest of the patients at the hospital would be treated for the release of harmful disincarnates. This was also accomplished through energy passes. He would also have private sessions of medical intuition once a month and private energy passes once a week. All was either supervised or done directly by Damo. Soon after his arrival, Marcel was told by some of the center's mediums that he was being troubled by spirits who had known him in past lives. Although initially disconcerting, this perspective proved to be very helpful, pointing him in the direction of very specific work he had to do to regain his stability.

From Mental Illness to Mediumship

After several weeks of medical intuition and dis-obsession, Marcel's periods of violent aggression stopped, as did his delusions. He then began studying Kardec's philosophy in the first books, "*The Spirits*" and "*The Mediums' Book*." Damo was continually monitoring Marcel's emotional stability, also his understanding of Kardecist philosophy. Damo could see, by indicators in Marcel's subtle energy field (aura), that Marcel was a medium with healing abilities. This became more evident as disincarnate entities causing his obsessing were liberated. Marcel needed more study to gain conceptual understanding of spiritual realms and the practice of mediumship. Marcel also needed to come to terms with how his prior lifetimes had contributed to the internal stresses of the present lifetime.

I met Marcel twice in 2003, after he had done a considerable amount of study and skill building as a medium, under the direct supervision of Damo. Marcel was then functioning as one member of a team of healing mediums, and was still taking a minimal dose of medications. Johann Grobler, a psychiatrist from South Africa traveling with me, asked Marcel: "Why does a person get possessed by a disincarnate entity?"

Marcel answered, "When the etheric body (a subtle energy field around the physical body) is weakened by stress or depression, spirits driven by negative emotions, like anger, greed, lust, addiction, fear and vengeance, can take possession of him or her. The weakened person is unable to over-ride the willfulness of the negative disincarnates, in this case and he or she is driven to irrational behaviors. The undeveloped spirits may come to hurt the person or his family, in response to hurt they felt in other lifetimes at the hand of that same individual. These entities get trapped in obsessing and part of releasing them is to help them be free to go on to their next step of development."

Marcel's current inner balance and peacefulness is obvious and clear testimony to his having successfully confronted his "demons." His healing depended on "inner transformation," called "reforma intima" in Portuguese, that necessitated his making amends for prior wrong-doing (acting in a way that is not compassionate to oneself or others) in this and other lifetimes. His dedication to be of service to others through healing is a central way he is making his amends.

The negative patterns of the mind brought about by obsession take time to heal. Marcel has been asked by Damo to stay for two years in Palmelo, to study Kardec and other Spiritist teachers, and continue his service work, receiving spiritual healing, and living a life in which stress is minimized. According to Damo, "This will completely restore his balance."

I had the opportunity to visit Marcel at the home he shares with his mother and father. The love that flowed among them all was palpable, and obviously contributed to Marcel's healing. The three reported that they had been through a lot of soul-searching together, including sharing the events from past-lives, where various difficulties had arisen among them, causing conflict that had continued into this lifetime. Marcel's reforma intima had involved all three of them resolving these issues and making a deeper commitment to treat each other with compassion, in brotherhood, that transcends the roles of this lifetime: as mother, father and son. I feel sure the simple diet, with plenty of Acerola juice (high in Vitamin C) also contributes to Marcel's healing.

When I first met Marcel he was ushering visitors as they prepared to have a personal session with Vania Damo, Damo's wife, who is gifted in automatic writing. (Dona Vania is one of the most well respected teachers in the community, as well as the main person who performs the service of automatic writing, to comfort those who want to communicate with loved ones who have died.) I had also watched Marcel giving "energy passes" during dis-obsessions at the hospital. At his present level of development he is learning to deliberately 'incorporate,' that is, allow a highly evolved disincarnate to use his body for a specific period of time, to transmit helpful information or do psychic healing.

Arnoldo, Marcel's father, has come to believe that the majority of cases of schizophrenia are caused by disincarnates possessing a person, or causing an individual to obsess. As he and his wife witnessed their son improving dramatically, they felt they had to accept the principles of Spiritism. Arnoldo told me, "I got back my son. I thought he might be gone forever." Even as Catholics, the family began believing in reincarnation and the necessity of making amends for mistakes in previous lifetimes. Like Marcel, they learned to strengthen their focus on peace and love, and control the images and thoughts in their minds, to deliberately be more positive. Kardec's Spiritism considers this discipline is essential to healing. It helps individuals separate from the negative influence of undeveloped disincarnates—and paves the way for those entities to be "educated," learning that they too are free to develop.

I asked Marcel, his mother and father, what they would want others to know about Marcel's healing, if they could address the world. His mother said, "What makes healing possible is our faith in God's goodness, and our ability to see life from new perspectives, getting over our prejudice against Spiritism." Both parents agreed, "The patient must actively participate in his healing through study and other activities of a Spiritist center, like Palmelo." Marcel said, "My story is concrete evidence that medication in combination with Spiritism work. You need both."

The Place and the People

Several people who live in Palmelo told me Palmelo has very positive geo-magnetic energies for promoting health. Many people come and live in Palmelo, as "outpatients," taking part in community activities without ever being in the hospital there. Anyone is free to come for dis-obsession, the study of the doctrine of Kardec in classrooms, and sessions of medical intuition, as well as psychic surgery for physical illnesses. A schedule of events is published and widely circulated so that visitors know the appropriate time and place for these events.

Sign on central building of "Centro Luz e Verdade":

Palmelo. Center for bringing balance to the physical, mental and spiritual. The only city in the world founded by Spiritists for Spiritism. Founded in 1929 as a foundation: Spiritist Center of Light and Truth.
"What is given freely will be transmitted for free."
A place of peace and love.
We welcome you.

Not only Damo and his wife, Vania, but all of the 50 to 220 mediums who assist the three thousand visitors coming to Palmelo each month for healing, volunteer their services. Salu, the director of the mental hospital, serving one hundred in-patients, also works for free. His wife, a teacher at the local elementary school, supports him and their two children.

In Palmelo, the community of mediums also create a background of loving attention and service. Their close-knit bonds were forged and tempered by years spent in training as mediums, working under the supervision of Mr. and Mrs. Damo. Inn keepers who tend to patients visiting for healing also have forged deep bonds through sharing the work of caring for the ill. Inn keepers who attend visitors and patients undergoing healing are mediums. They supervise the care of the Center's patients by managing meals, providing colonics when necessary, and leading group discussions and study groups at the Inns.

The fact that Palmelo is a small, relatively remote village in the countryside also contributes to the strength of the community. All neighbors as well as co-workers. Transportation around town is by foot or bicycle. People are often outside, sitting in chairs in front of their homes, greeting passersby. The garden park, occupying a full city block in front of Euripedes Barsanulfo Hospital, is a riot of color with numerous beds of diverse flowers, interrupted only by trees, a walkway and park benches, where one can sit and talk with a friend. Patients in the hospital enjoy coming to the park to sit, and visit with residents or with visitors walking by.

Phrase repeatedly found in Palmelo's newsletters:
"Read Kardec to understand Christ"

The members of the Center of Light and Truth teach classes on Kardec and discuss the Christian principles embedded in Kardec's books. They recognize that those coming to Palmelo for healing have often lived lives where they have been hurtful to others, and self-destructive, eating poorly, overindulging in alcohol and drugs, and not taking care of themselves. For these people, healing involves a *"re-orientation"* where one recognizes the necessity of purifying one's body, emotions, and thoughts. Classroom discussions and readings shared at the inns and in the psychiatric hospital give visitors the opportunity to come to terms with the idea that this life is for the purpose of spiritual evolution. If a person chooses to believe this, he or she then sees the necessity of further study of the components of spiritual evolution, and how to go about that process. The members of the community serve as models, as they are involved with the discipline of study and being of service to others through volunteer work.

Those visiting Palmelo will often hear that pain or disease is an alarm clock, to enable one to wake up to the meaning of life in general and their mission in particular. With time in this quiet village to reflect, one may come to believe that expressing brotherly love is the highest priority of life, and essential to healing. Damo reflects on healing this way: "We have to cure organ pathology from the inside-out. Not from simply taking medications to obscure symptoms, or radiation and surgery to do way with the affected organ that is the end result of an inner cause. That is a way of cure from the outside-in, which never stops to analyze nor pull out the roots of the symptoms." With this in mind, many people coming for healing find that their life needs radical transformation.

Marcel, like others, had to become conscious of why he became mentally ill, then make amends for past transgressions, and change his life to effect the cure. "It's up to each person how long that process takes," says Damo.

I'll never forget watching Damo move past the mediums performing group dis-obsessions. Up and down the line he went, observing what the mediums were doing, helping patients who might be feeling weak or in need of special help. In his gruff way, Damo would almost shout—"Seja Jesus abençoado!" (Jesus be Blessed), "Gloria!," "Firmeza por caridade!" (Please maintain your focus), or just "Firme!" (Concentrate! Focus!) In this way he consistently helped the mediums to stay focused, and strengthen their connection to the highly evolved spiritual beings. Focus on channeling only the energy of the most evolved spirits is, of course essential —especially during the occasion of a dis-obsession, where one is also liberating negatively motivated spirits, and helping them move away away from harming human beings.

No matter how magical the healing sounds, Palmelo's healers don't offer magic cures. Damo puts it quite bluntly, "*Palmelo only cures when one's debts are paid and you deserve to be healed.*" In these terms, going to Palmelo to be healed is an extremely expensive proposition. Money can not pay your way, and a powerful healer can not heal you. Instead, you, the one seeking healing, must do the work of making amends for past wrong-doing, through life times. This kind of healing demands one's total resources of dedication, diligence, humility, and courage. One must face prior experiences one might rather forget, as well as the unknown. The process demands you give up who you pretend to be, when you pretend the darkness of your past doesn't exist. The goal is to re-orient your life so you can realize your positive inner potential.

A wall-hanging at Palmelo's Center

"You recognize a true Spiritist by their moral transformation and the effort they make to dominate their negative tendencies."

— Allan Kardec

Chapter Six

Busca Vida

Where Palmelo is a demonstration of traditional Kardecist Spiritism, "Busca Vida," Center of the Research of Life, a healing center in the suburbs of Brasilia, is an example of Kardecist principles at work in a contemporary healing center. They offer the following healing modalities:

- Orientation to "How the Mind Works".
- Electromagnetic Rejuvenation Devices.
- Meditation.
- Yoga, T'ai Chi, Chi Kung classes.

Marco de Albuquerque is the director of "Busca Vida." Marco has completed training in Silva Mind Control, (learning to use the mind in a positive way), and Reiki, a form of light-touch spiritual healing from Japan. She has also been a student of both Kardec's books and the channeled writings from H. Blavatsky and Alice Bailey, (both of whom are said to have transmitted teachings from highly evolved spiritual masters). The resources for healing she offers concentrate on a number of electromagnetic devices for rejuvenation, inventions of Paul Laussac, a Brazilian engineer, used in combination with older forms of health management practiced at Palmelo.

Laussac worked primarily as a healer for eighteen years. Beginning in 1959, when he was eighteen years old, Laussac trained with a Catholic priest to strengthen his skills in healing and de-possession. Later, as an engineer and inventor, Laussac investigated radionics, psychotronics and parapsychology, traveling to sixty-nine countries to participate in research on psi-phenomena. In 1977, Laussac began putting together electronic devices to stimulate the effects of energy and magnetic healing passes one receives at centers like Palmelo. Laussac met Marco de Albuquerque in 1998, when she was exploring the range of alternative therapies. Since that time, Busca Vida has been integrating Laussac's new rejuvenation devices into the program they offer. Busca Vida is gathering data about the effectiveness of these devices and intends to become a training center for those who want to learn how to use the apparatuses in healing centers and hospitals around the world.

Several highly developed mediums I spoke with both in Palmelo and Abadiania believe that Busca Vida is located within a large area in central Brazil, that has a measurably strong geo-magnetic energy field, especially helpful for helping people find peace and healing. (Palmelo is also in this field.) These same Brazilians believe this area may physically seed the rest of the world with renewed vision and energy. This idea is an echo from the past. In 1840, Dom Bosco, a Catholic priest, foretold that a great civilization will be born between the 15th and 20th parallels in Brazil. A small altar, dedicated to Dom Bosco, was the first edifice built when ground was broken for the city of Brasilia in the mid-20th century. Brasilia is now the capital of Brazil, housing the central governmental offices, and exhibiting some of the most beautifully engineered, modern architecture in the world.

Busca Vida, a fifteen-minute drive from Brasilia, looks like a small health care facility one might find in the USA or Europe. The largest building is a single-level structure divided into five treatment rooms, two offices, and a reception area. There are also two free-standing, one room buildings that are used by individual teachers for classes in meditation, yoga, Chi-Kung, and T'ai Chi. Another single-level structure is sometimes used to house visiting health professionals (by special permission only). There are approximately two acres of grounds that will, in the future, be used for small cabins (yet to be constructed) for students and other guests.

When a person first comes to Busca Vida he/she spends an hour or so with Marco—at no charge. They discuss treatment goals and the visitor listens to Marco's presentation on "How the Mind Works." Quoting the words of many teachers and healers, past and present, using graphic illustrations on transparencies projected on a large screen, Marco makes it clear that each client must actively participate in his/her healing process. Marco says that changing negative thinking to positive thinking is essential to healing—as is a lifestyle that includes exercise, meditation, good nutrition and adequate rest—nurturing a purification of the emotional, and physical body as well as the thinking patterns.

> "A disease process is evidence that something is amiss in the workings of the mind, and that is where the power to effect a change resides."
> — David Hawkins, MD

Like other Spiritists, Marco is convinced that we have more than our five senses: tasting, hearing, seeing, touching, and smelling. She includes intuition as a sixth sense, and suggests that other senses can be developed to facilitate self-healing and expand awareness.

The process of healing and rejuvenation she offers to clients of Busca Vida seem to have all the components of a Spiritist Center like Palmelo, with one exception. Laussac's innovative electromagnetic healing devices take the place of energy passes and psychic surgery. Both Marco and Laussac maintain that the correct use of these electromagnetic devices effectively resolve problems of possession and obsession. Otherwise, personal consultation, prayer, study, making amends for past transgressions, and re-orienting one's life to spiritual growth and a healthy life style, are considered essential. This combining new technologies of Energy Medicine with alternative therapies and principles of Kardec's Spiritism, puts Busca Vida in a position of pioneering a whole new kind of Spiritist Center.

Marlene's Cancer Treatment

Marlene was brought to Busca Vida in March, 2003, by her brother, Dr. Idalmo. She was fifty-nine years old. Recent X-rays had shown she had cancer that had metastasized to her pancreas, stomach, and liver. Her oncologist in Brazil said she had three months to live. He prescribed radiation, chemotherapy and immediate surgery to extend her life, but promised no cure. Marlene decided to forgo these mainstream approaches and try Laussac's devices for rejuvenation.

Six months after Marlene started treatment at Busca Vida she had no cancer in her body. This is documented by X-rays and blood tests, analyzed by both her oncologist and Dr. Idalmo. As of October, 2003, Marlene was making plans for her future. She continues to maintain her health by going to Busca Vida for two treatments each week.

The twenty US dollars cost per treatment is a nominal fee used to maintain the Center and pay the office staff. Like other Spiritist Centers, Busca Vida is not a for profit business.

Dr. Idalmo, Marlene's brother, was licensed as a physician and surgeon in 1969 in Brazil. He extended his training to become a certified Naturopath in 1973, then a Homeopath in 1998. From his studies, he has come to believe that cancer originates in the following way:

"Cancer often grows out of a psychological conflict and/or physical trauma. The trauma registers in the cerebral cortex. The brain then activates the cells in the affected area in abnormal ways. When there is physical damage, e.g. a cut or bruising from a fight or accident, some cells die off, and then the area is reconstructed with abnormal cells. Where there is psychological damage, e.g. a betrayal of trust or loss of intimacy or power, the same thing is set in motion, with abnormal cells replacing the cells that were in the most affected area. Instead of attacking the abnormal cancer cells, it is better to help the body/mind let go of the conflict that strengthened the possibility of abnormal cell growth. In this way we address the root cause of the problem, and stop it from creating any more abnormal cells in the future."

The following page shows a diagram to map this theory. It illustrates that a stressful experience can lead to a degree of depression that registers in the limbic system, the part of the brain concerned with basic emotion, hunger and sex. This in turn activates the hypothalamus, a control center concerned with autonomic functions. The next link in the chain of events is a signal to the pituitary gland, the master endocrine gland that next depresses the whole endocrine system including the working of the immune system. This lays the groundwork for abnormal cells to be created, which may manifest as cancer.

Marlene is a deeply religious, strong and generous person, with a well-disciplined ability to focus. She could easily understand Marco's initial

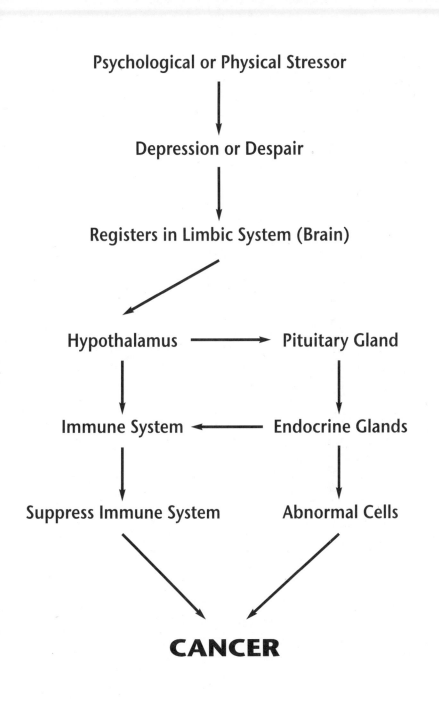

presentation, the need to think positively, and to forgive those who had hurt her in the past. Marlene committed herself to the necessary inner work and was willing to explore using the electromagnetic devices, despite the fact that they are used for research purposes only. The clinic makes no promises for cures.

Laussac's Electromagnetic Devices

The first of Laussac's devices she learned to use was the "Pineal Trainer," "PT," a "trans-cranial electro-stimulator" (TCES). Such electrostimulators have been used for decades in Russia, where they have found them to be highly effective in the treatment of addiction, depression and anxiety. More than one hundred clinical trials that have been reported in medical papers about TCES of various kinds. The National Insititutes of Health are currently funding research on these devices in the USA[1].

Laussac's PT sends an extremely low frequency electric current from one electrode placed on the third eye between the eyebrows to another electrode, placed at the base of the skull in a groove where the spine meets the head. Laussac maintains that the extremely low frequency electrical stimulation passing between these two points synchronizes all four quadrants of the brain, and ultimately lowers the brain wave frequency to "delta" (0.5 Hertz). This low brain wave pattern allows access into the deepest resources of the mind that are inaccessible when the brain wave pattern is in a more ordinary, higher frequency, state. He reports that the PT accelerates the process of releasing negative beliefs and attitudes and awakens potentials for self-healing, speed learning, and self-actualization. Laussac believes the PT elevates people to a higher level of consciousness, which is usually only attained after years of meditation and discipline of the mind.

> "It is possible for a lifelong affliction to heal rapidly with a mere shift of attitude; but although this shift may seem to occur in a split second, it may take years of inner preparation."
>
> — David Hawkins, MD

Marlene took the PT home and used it by herself every day to help her relax before sleep. She also used it at Busca Vida, in conjunction with other healing devices. Once the device is placed on one's head, the treatment involves relaxing for thirty minutes while listening to an audiotape of positive, uplifting messages. These affirmations are previously taped by the client, in his/her own voice. Marlene said that the current running through her brain was painless; the treatment deeply relaxing.

Laussac agrees with Idalmo's concept of both the psychological origins of cancer, and the physiological sequence leading to abnormal cell growth. He added, "We don't need any devices or energetic passes when we have the power to heal ourselves. But, this power is dormant in most of us. That is why most of us need to be jump-started by rejuvenation devices. By stimulating the brain with the PT the negative sequence of thinking and patterns of negative emotion can be stopped, and replaced with positive thoughts, catalyzing states of inner peace to replace depression.

After learning how to use the PT, Marlene had treatments with other devices also invented by Laussac for rejuvenation. One such treatment involved her resting on a bed inside a one inch wide metal frame on the perimeter of the bed. This frame contains electrical wiring that emits a particular inaudible "vibration." It is a non-invasive treatment that Marlene again found to be deeply relaxing. Laussac claims the *"Magnetic Portal,"* re-aligns the magnetic fields of the body. He described why we need such realignment: Energy fields radiating from microwaves, radios, transformers from high-tension power lines, cell phones, computers, cable and TV fill the atmosphere, and destabilize the magnetic field of the body. Our cells respond by losing the memory of how each one is programmed to function and reproduce. The loss of memory may result in the construction of abnormal cells or cancer cells. Laussac designed the magnetic portal in order to re-establish harmony in the inherent memory of each cell as well as between the cells. He believes this creates harmony in the magnetic fields of the body as a whole.

Another device Marlene used was Laussac's *"Cellular Rejuvenator."* She sat on a plastic chair, her feet resting on a glass plate on the floor of the device, her hands holding a glass ball just above her lap. When the rejuvenator is turned on the electrical current moves into the glass ball, impregnates the contents with energy, and thus generates a highly ionizing gas, containing an approximately equal number of positive ions and electrons. Within the glass ball are specific gases, minerals and other elements no longer present in our diet, but essential to preserving life and health.

Painlessly, this "bio-plasmic" gaseous energy is transmitted into the body of the client by "inducted" (not direct) electricity. Laussac believes that this process restores the vitality of both the physical and subtle bodies. The inducted low amperage of electricity promotes beneficial biological transmutation. (He says that higher amperage of electricity cannot accomplish this.) Although the typical treatment is twenty-five minutes per day, the cellular rejuvenator is used for up to an hour, three times a day, for people with cancer, AIDS, or Lupus.

Laussac says his "*Thymus Gland Activator*" increases the strength of the immune system to very high levels in a very short period of time by sending minute particles of minerals and specific intensities of light toward the Thymus gland. When it is activated, the thymus gland produces more T-4 Lymphocytes, as well as NK cells. These are the first cells the body produces to combat any kind of invaders, like viruses or bacteria. Most people feel no sensations at all during this kind of treatment. Sensitive people, like Marlene, report feeling a pleasant flow of beneficial energy entering their bodies.

The Laussac devices to be used on any particular day with Marlene were chosen through muscle-testing (refer back to Chapter Four for an explanation. This same technique was used to define Levels of Consciousness). This is a well-researched technique that allows a practitioner, like Marco, to communicate with the "inner wisdom" of the patient, that part of an individual that intrinsically knows what he/she needs at any particular point. (The extent to which muscle-testing can be effectively used to bring forth the hidden wisdom of the body/mind is explained very clearly by psychiatrist, David Hawkins, MD, Ph.D., in his book "*Power versus Force*".)

Replacing Energy Passes

Laussac contends that his rejuvenation devices are all similar to the energy passes of mediums in that the specifically calibrated electrical energy of the devices nurtures the body, reminding the cells how to work in harmony with each other, thus contributing to re-establishing health and wellbeing. Used in conjunction with lowering brain wave patterns, a patient will begin feeling an increase in inner peace and positivity. The quality that makes Laussac's devices different from treatment by mediums is their *consistency*. Human beings are subject to varying moods, emotional reactions, and unconscious drives that can distort or diminish the power of healing work. Devices engineered to be steady in their output of energy, and finely calibrated to maintain a specific amperage, do not have these human variables, and are thus more dependable. Also, mediums, over the course of their work with patients, often absorb the negativity, or illness of their patients. Electronic devices are not vulnerable in this way.

Electromagnetic devices for medical treatments have been in use for more than one hundred years. In the 1930's and 1940's, two researchers, an American, Royal Rife, and a Russian, Georges Lakhovsky, demonstrated that the electromagnetic devices each invented were over ninety percent successful in the treatment of cancer in plants, animals and human beings. Unfortunately, their successful protocols were obscured by the more popular bio-chemical paradigm and its search for the "magic bullet" to win the war against cancer. Only now, at the beginning of the twenty-first century, (when we have failed to find the magic bullet) are North Americans and Europeans and Russians, returning to develop and apply the innovative technologies first researched by Rife and Lakhovsky.

Laussac and Marco suggest that treatment time is cut by at least 50% for all manner of diseases when a patient uses Laussac's devices. Why? Because the patients work on themselves and are treated in an atmosphere that supports lowering brain wave patterns to facilitate deep relaxation and connection to inner wisdom. When patients understand this at the beginning of their treatment, they gain confidence in the treatment they receive, and are more able to cooperate, as well as be hopeful.

"Changing mental attitudes is essential to creating change in life."
— William James, psychologist

In 1978 Laussac spent three days with Chico Xavier, referred to in Chapter Two as a living saint. Xavier was recognized as one of the most important leaders of Spiritism in Brazil. He died in 2001. Laussac asked Xavier for his perspective on the value of his electromagnetic devices for healing, which he calls "Quantum Vibrational Therapy" (QVT).

Laussac reports that Xavier replied, "*Your work is an avenue for the future. It is a field of science that will transform medicine and healing. Even the best of Spiritist healing, energy passes, will take second place behind the efficient therapy that comes with your apparatuses.*"

This suggests that electromagnetic devices in general, and Laussac's inventions in particular, may have a very important role in making future improvements in the way medicine is practiced. It does appear that QVT is a very important perspective that is making a contribution to our understanding of what creates health and what rejuvenates the body. More research needs to be done to define the parameters of its effectiveness, along with research on other devices under development by other bio-medical engineers around the world. (If you are interested in knowing more, see books and articles by James Oschman, PhD.) Both Laussac and Marco look forward to the time more research studies on QVT will demonstrate the length of treatment necessary for each specific disease, and the effectiveness of using the range of devices. They are currently applying for research grants for this purpose.

Vital to all Healing

Despite the fact that electromagnetic devices appear to offer great potential, they are not a "magic bullet." As Damo emphatically stated in Palmelo, there are other components vital to healing. Energy healing is only one part. How effective would the treatment at Busca Vida be without the wisdom, compassion, and love of Marco and her assistants? (When I asked Marco why, at 74 years of age, she is still managing the center, she said, "I need a way to give my love to people.") The nurturing community, a component of all the Spiritist centers I have visited, must be a significant part of the healing they offer. At Busca Vida it seemed that all the patients had formed a close connection to Marco and the other attendants who greet them at the door when they enter, inquiring about their health and well being. Always, they are asked, "How are you?," offered a hug and a kiss on both cheeks (as is the custom in Brazil,) and helped in and out of the treatment rooms. Patients who also participate in classes, e.g. T'ai Chi or Yoga, come to know fellow patients in a positive environment. Weekly meditations provide another avenue to reinforce the sense of brotherhood in this world and with evolved spirits in other dimensions. The spirits of the highly evolved masters Marco invokes during prayer and meditation, along with the peaceful natural surroundings of Busca Vida, may also be essential factors in the successful healing patients experience there.

We cannot lose sight of the fact, echoed through contemporary researchers, that it is essential that the patient be willing to apply what he/she learns. Each patient *has to* re-orient his/her life to being positive, forgiving and compassionate. If abnormal cell growth is first initiated by a psychological stressor, as Idalmo believes, then the way out of the imbalance must also include rooting out the psychological disturbance. This demands a high degree of self-responsibility, sometimes giving up old patterns of both thinking and behaving, to radically change one's life.

The expectation that cure *can* happen is also a vital component of healing. Marco accomplishes this in her first session with a patient, when she compassionately receives them, describes how the mind works, and how they can participate in their rejuvenation. The emotion of hope in the patient, catalyzes biochemical responses in the body: the positive emotion is transmitted to the limbic system setting off a chain reaction in the brain, eventually stimulating both the immune and endocrine systems, assisting them to work to restore balance to the normal functioning of the cells. This must happen to lay the groundwork for the remission of cancerous growths.

Although Busca Vida is exploring innovative protocols, there are still many components of Kardecist Spiritist healing work, which may be components of any healing process, anywhere.

Chapter Seven

Centro

One of the strongest Spiritist community centers I visited is in San Paulo. Founded in 1977, "Centro" is housed in several adjoining buildings, close to the downtown financial district, separated from the main street only by a high wall. If you didn't know what you were looking for, Centro's small sign could be easily missed among the busy storefronts. Behind the non-descript metal door are:

- Regular interviews with social work assistants.
- Classes to study the writings of Kardec and Xavier.
- A school for training mediums.
- Large rooms where healers work on visitors wanting healing.
- An assembly hall for talks and attending automatic writing.
- Two large kitchens to supply a café and food for the poor.
- A bazaar for selling used clothing and household items.
- Treatment rooms for visiting doctors who volunteer their time.
- A pharmacy donating free supplements and fulfilling prescriptions.
- Classes to prepare for family life and the care of infants.
- Consultation rooms where professionals volunteer time to advise individuals needing financial and legal help.
- Offices for administration.

What makes this center so strong in its community feeling must be that it was founded by a family, and, more than twenty years later, is managed by that same family. Currently, the Executive Director is a woman, her nephew is the vice-president, and various aunts, uncles, nieces and nephews participate in one role or another. The generation that founded the center also coordinated with one of the best mediums Brazil has ever had, a teacher and trainer of mediums, and an author, Martha G. Thomaz. When I asked the Vice President, "What makes your Center unique?," he answered, "We respect each human being, no matter what he or she believes. We don't proselytize. Instead, we educate the person, sharing our love and generosity, while maintaining our focus on Kardec. We feel that gives us stability."

Although they receive over eight hundred people on Saturdays, their busiest day, the center is small, with limited resources to receive international guests. They have asked me to maintain their anonymity. I'll call them, "Centro Consolação e Inspiração" (the Center for Consolation and Inspiration) or "Centro" to protect their identity and location. However, following below are recently collected impressive statistics revealing their successes.

At Centro the kitchen and janitorial help and one social worker who is a part-time supervisor, are the only people who are paid. (The government insists that this licensed social worker be part of the paid staff.) All others are volunteers, and no fees are charged for services rendered. In 2002, ninety-one volunteers were working as teachers. There were one thousand and twenty-four students. In the first three months of 2002, five thousand seven hundred people came for energy passes. Approximately one thousand people came to get messages from the departed from Centro's mediums doing automatic writing, and of those, six hundred received the requested messages. The whole organization functions on a budget of approximately $8500 per month, donated by independent people.

Tania: Preventive Medicine

Tania, a fictional name, was in a difficult and painful situation. Her husband, Luis, had been recently killed in a factory accident, leaving her alone and destitute, to care for their two children, ten and fourteen. Her father had died two years before and her aging mother was infirm and lived with her. Tania feared for their survival. She had been feeling extremely weary for months before she came to the "Centro Consolação e Inspiração."

While her children were in school, Tania and her mother went by bus to the Centro on a Thursday afternoon. On entering, they happily accepted the invitation to free bread and soup. They were hungry, denying themselves food, so that the children could be adequately fed. Then, Tania was interviewed by an interning social worker, Ana. Ana filled out a 3" by 5" card with Tania's name, briefly noting what she believed Tania told her she needed: physical and/or spiritual help, and/or energy passes. She checked boxes related to specific life problems Tania reported, all abbreviated by an initial: H for HIV positive, AL for alcoholism, X for drug dependency, W for suicidal feelings, C for cancer, D for physical depression or obsession, AN for aneurysm, and M for natural medium not yet trained to handle the gift. She noted that Tania had been experiencing pain in her chest. Rather than in a specific diagnosis, Ana briefly noted the organ Tania said was causing a problem, and what kind of pain or problem she reported. (In this way, Ana is not "diagnosing" or "suggesting treatment, " a task reserved for medical personnel.) Instead, she is reporting issues, and inviting Tania to participate in activities of the Center. Ana is also not encouraging Tania to think of herself as "a person with heart problems," rather "a person who currently has some pain in her heart."

Ana invited Tania to use the resources of the Center by coming for five treatments of energy passes and a medical exam with volunteer cardiologist, prior to coming back for another interview. She then gave the card back to Ana to use for identification when she returned, and made sure she was given a number, so she would be recognized in the computer system. Tania's name would be kept anonymously in the system. Ana's records would not reflect any details of Tania's personal situation by name, only that a person, identified by a specific number, had come in for a particular kind of assistance. When she received the energy passes, a Centro volunteer would initial and date the treatment, on the 3 X 5 card.

Tania turned the card over in her hand, noticing the message at the bottom: "Attention: Spiritual treatment does not free you from the need for medical treatment." She knew it was important for her to see one of the Center's volunteer physicians about her physical health. The message confirmed her thinking.

Tania's mother, Claudia, was also interviewed. Ana noted that Claudia needed both a physical exam and spiritual assistance. She was lonely, possibly in need of supplements in her diet.

Although interviewers did not keep records on specific people attending Centro, they did make general notes on the age and educational level of who came for assistance, and what kinds of problems, and what kinds of successes were reported. This allowed the interviewers to gather general statistics. They were also responsible for establishing the level of financial need of visitors. Tania was told she had to provide written proof that her children had received their inoculations before they could take advantage of any of the free medical consultations at Centro (dentistry, psychological counseling, hearing screening, acupuncture, and physiotherapy).

Before they left, both Tania and Claudia were advised to return on the following Monday, between 1-5pm. At that time, they could again receive free soup and bread, as well as consultations with a physician/homeopath, and a cardiologist. If remedies, medication or supplements were prescribed, the pharmacy would also be open to provide them. Over one thousand prescriptions are donated to the poor at Centro each month. Since Tania had adequate evidence demonstrating she makes less than 600 Real per month ($192), she was also given free food to take home with her: flour, rice, beans, oil, sugar, and some fresh vegetables.

On their way out of "Centro" Claudia noticed young pregnant women entering a classroom, and some older women, heading upstairs. "Where are they going?," she asked Ana. "These poor pregnant girls are learning what they need to do to care for themselves during pregnancy, and to care for their newborns. They are also being prepared for childbirth. This is practical information about the need for good food, adequate rest, refraining from drinking alcohol, and strengthening exercises. About fifty-five young women attend the classes each month. Over ninety percent of them are illiterate (as noted by the interviewers during initial conversations)."

Ana took Tania and Claudia to an upstairs room. Smiling, she said, "Here are our busy-bees." There sat eight older adult women, chatting together, as they knitted and sewed various articles to be given to the new mothers for their newborns. Brightly colored cloth was stacked neatly on shelves. Three hours each Monday, Thursday and Friday afternoon the workshop was open for those who wanted to make layettes, or learn how to sew. Clearly it was just as much a social group, as a workshop. Recipes were traded at the same time needles were being threaded. Claudia was especially happy to see women her own age, visiting cheerfully while they contributed something useful to those in need. She said she had felt so useless lately, unable to afford anything to help her daughter and grandchildren, except the food off her own plate.

Deeply moved by the loving, generous community feeling at the Centro, both Tania and Claudia also became interested in what would be asked of them in the "Basic Course." Attending this course was required of all people who regularly use Centro's resources and attend activities. They both felt suspicious of the possibility of religious indoctrination. They didn't want to give up their affiliation with their Catholic Church. They found the course provides an opportunity to discuss the significance of spiritual values and principles to live by. It also reflected on the reasoning behind the existence of God and spiritual realms, contemplating how spirits can meaningfully interact with human beings. The Basic Course lasts thirty weeks, from April to December, with a two hour class, once a week.

Since Tania's husband had unexpectedly died, she no longer felt sure that God existed. "How could there be a loving God if He has taken my husband and only source of support?," she wondered. "How could He leave me alone to care for two children and an elderly mother? Have I done something wrong to deserve this? Am I being punished?"

Claudia also had unresolved questions on her mind: "Where did my husband go when he died? What will happen to me when I die? Will I be reunited with my husband? Will I be judged by saints in heaven for my wrong-doings? Does Hell exist? Is dying a lonely experience?" She wondered if the Basic Course would help her with these kinds of questions. She wanted to find peace of mind before she died.

That night, at home, bellies finally full with a substantial dinner of rice and beans, Tania and Claudia pored over the Schedule of Activities at the Centro. They noted that three times a week they could go to the meeting of "automatic writing" and possibly receive messages from their loved ones who had died. Several trained mediums at the Centro were said to know how to receive specific messages from disincarnates. Tania also made note that Saturday evening would be pizza night, celebrating the birthdays of everyone born in the month of April. This would be a good opportunity to introduce the children to the community. Perhaps they would also become interested in attending the youth group, Saturday afternoons.

Four days after Tania and Claudia's first visit, they returned for consultations with doctors. Both were given nutritional supplements, and Tania was put on homeopathic heart medication, which soon eased her symptoms and helped her to feel revitalized. She also received free legal advice that helped her confront her husband's place of employment seeking extra support for her family. She had previously not been aware of her legal rights. She also received help in applying to the Brazilian government's welfare programs.

Gradually, over the course of the next few months, the whole family became involved in the Centro's community activities. For two months, they were provided with basic food supplies. When Tania found work, and was able to bring home money, she no longer needed the donated food from Centro. Claudia joined the women's sewing circles. Both Claudia and Tania felt uplifted, empowered, and held by the warm circle of love in the community. It helped ease the pain of no longer having their husbands for support and companionship.

After six months, Tania and Claudia were both attending many activities of the center each week. They came regularly for energy passes. The Basic Course answered many spiritual questions never addressed fully in Catholicism. They still loved the freedom to attend Catholic Mass and high celebrations at Easter and Christmas at their beloved church. They never felt it was disloyal to their community at the Centro. In fact, they saw that many others who frequented Centro also continued to attend a church, mosque or synagogue. "Clearly," they thought, "the community of the Centro is more vital because of this diversity and ecumenism."

Their fears of being indoctrinated by a cult that might take them away from their Catholic beliefs, had proven to be unfounded. On the contrary, the Basic Course opened them to think through new perspectives without making any demands on what they *should* believe. Both Tania and Claudia felt free to contemplate new possibilities: perhaps reincarnation does exist...it appears that Science can show evidence of reincarnation...perhaps hell exists within us psychologically when we are full of anxiety, fear or envy...perhaps we should take charge of our own lives and put ourselves more deliberately on a path of evolution, where we become happier people, as we are more compassionate with others. After two months of the courses, they had been introduced to many new concepts and were in the process of deciding how they wanted change their prior understanding of the meaning of life itself, as well as the role religion plays in their lives.

"Spiritism is the scientific, philosophical, and moral basis of all religions."

— Allan Kardec

They had lively discussions with their two teenagers, who were also interested in exploring new perspectives. The children were talking about current events in their schools. As part of the Basic Course, Claudia and Tania were also reading and thinking about biologists, philosophers and researchers, people presently in the news, who were discussing the energy of all living things. Current research supported the view that energy passes have a scientific basis[2]. Movies, like "Crouching Tiger, Hidden Dragon" (2000), where two female martial artists use paranormal abilities in the battle against negative forces, were a topic of discussion in the classroom. They talked about the drama between the impulse to brotherhood and compassion and the need to survive, deceive or fight for selfish gain. Everything they were being exposed to in reading Kardec pointed to the necessity for ethical behavior, and brotherhood as the way to make spiritual progress, become happier, and contribute to peace in the world.

After six months, Claudia had made many friends with the older women her age. Her social life outside the immediate family became centered in Centro's activities to benefit the poor, sewing with the other "busy bees." As Tania became more independent, working each day, she still relied on the friendship and emotional support of the Centro's community. One of her children also decided to attend youth activities. The youth group discussed relevant questions of the day: AIDS, sexuality, finding your own values, and your own self-expression. How to live your life without harming others. Thus, the community nurtured each one in the family, with continual growth and deepening peace of mind.

For Claudia and Tania, one of the most powerful aspects of this on-going community life was hearing the stories of other community members. A team of six college students had been attending various activities at the Centro to complete a report for their Sociology class, on how Centro is organized. According to the director of Centro, the young people were so impressed and inspired by the loving compassion in action that they saw—

all of them had decided to continue visiting weekly as volunteers: making soup in the kitchen, working in the pharmacy, visiting the elderly who were unable to come to the Centro, also attending classes.

After receiving energy passes, Tania and Claudia would go to the snack bar at the Centro. This was the best place to hear news and chat. One woman, Elsie, ninety-nine years old, (referred to in Chapter Two,) continued to come at least twice a month for energy passes. She believed it was the spiritual healing that kept her strong enough to continue working five days a week as an editor. Two parents told of their child, formerly wild with "hyperactivity," who had become quieter and is now capable of participating in normal classroom activities, since receiving energy passes.

Cleide and Her Son: Confronting Cancer

Cleide, a social psychologist, had just completed her masters degree in the Science of Religion, and published her thesis, "A Eterna Busca da Cura" (The Eternal Search for Healing). In it she reflects on her own healing from kidney cancer, as well as her son's death from cancer of the stomach. Cleide's cancer was diagnosed early enough that careful surgical removal of the left kidney had stopped the malignancy from spreading to the rest of her body. Her oncologist had told her the cancer was two years old, and Cleide felt sure that the cancer had started at the same time she was in an extremely emotionally stressful situation. She made a promise to resolve any issues left over from this emotional situation, in the belief that it would prevent the recurrence of the cancer.

Cleide found a Spiritist psychotherapist who frequented Centro, to help her confront and work through the emotional and spiritual issues that she felt were still unresolved. She read a book by Lawrence Le Shan, "How Cancer is a Point of Transformation," and came to believe that all disease has a psychosomatic component. This further inspired her to attend activities at the Centro, to devote more time and effort to her inner transformation, and to support others as best she could.

"It is not the disease that must be exclusively treated, but the person and his/her history that harbored the disease," Cleide said. One of her teachers, an Argentinian psychoanalyst, Pichon Rivieri, had researched the origins of cancer for forty years. He concluded that 78% of all cancers originate in an extremely stressful emotional situation.

Cleide told Tania, "The function of Kardecist Spiritism is to restore hope, and the feeling of gratitude for life. As you meditate and pray, your intuition grows, as well. Then, you can more plainly see what caused the inner conflict that nurtured the seeds of illness in the first place, and release it." Tania wondered if her heart trouble began when her husband died and she felt the loss of his love.

"I studied the results of community members at the Centro," Cleide continued. "Eighty-seven percent told me they experienced an improvement of their condition. Seventy percent of the people I interviewed had great improvement and definite cure of their problem. I believe that the main factor for cure was *trust*—trust in the healer who transmits energy and confidence in the strength of the energy that is transmitted."

Tania had noticed that the mediums who do the energy passes at Centro seemed to have a special harmony among them. All the mediums have to concentrate on exactly the same thing at the same time. The belief Spiritists have is that the potential healing power is dissipated when the healers don't focus on the same thing or get distracted. Further, sharing the same theoretical foundation of healing, and respect for this specific type of Spiritism is believed to assist the healers to stay in harmony. When the person coming for healing is also taking responsibility for his/her inner transformation, Spiritists believe, you have an ideal situation to promote healing. Both Tania and Claudia were feeling more and more trust in the power of the energy passes at Centro, because each of them had more self-confidence and physical well being.

Cleide described a personal situation in which she explored the effects of healing on her son, as well. She told Tania that when he was twenty-three, his abdomen suddenly became very swollen, and he was diagnosed with cancer. Unfortunately, in his case, the cancer was very advanced. His doctors did not recommend surgery. According to Cleide, he had spiritual healings that helped cure his spiritual problems, but his body did not heal. She said that for nine months he examined his life intensely, and was able to deal with his physical pain caused by the cancer. By the time of his death, she believed he was at peace with answers he had found through Spiritism regarding the death process and to what level he would be able to evolve. Cleide said her son believed his body was just the shell of his spirit and that his spirit would go on living, in other more subtle forms, while it continued to evolve. She felt that the Centro had opened many doors for him, "The Centro helped us work through our pre-conceived notions, to embrace a more holistic path, to become more integrated in body, mind and spirit."

She felt that she had also learned how to help guide her son, in his last hours of this life, to make his passing as positive as possible. She believed that, because of this, he had a very peaceful passage out of his body. She was also able to ease her profound grief with the comfort of knowing that he had truly been at peace with himself at the end of his life.

It was comforting to Tania and her mother, that professionals, like Cleide, attended Spiritist activities at the Centro to learn, grow, heal, and be of service to others in need of help. There were others taking classes who were doctors, dentists, social workers, psychologists, and engineers who obviously valued what Centro had to offer. These same people often became qualified to perform energy passes for those coming for healing.

Chapter Eight

The Brazilian Federation of Spiritists of San Paulo (FEESP)

The Brazilian Federation of Spiritists of San Paulo State (FEESP) is located in the heart of downtown San Paulo. FEESP is a hub of tremendous activity. Although it does not have the intimacy of small community, like "Centro," the extent of its resources is impressive. Two thousand trained mediums volunteer their services. This allows FEESP to remain staffed and open from 8am to 10pm everyday, with a full schedule of activities. Each day, one thousand books are sold through the bookstore, the busiest in all of San Paulo. In 2002, FEESP had fourteen thousand adults and nine thousand youth in classes.

FEESP offers social services that are similar to other Spiritist Centers as well as Outreach:

- Healing sessions, Basic classes, and Training for mediumship and healing. (Each day four thousand people come to receive energy passes and three thousand attend classes.)

- Soup Kitchen and Food Distribution. (FEESP serves two hundred bowls of soup each day to the poor, and gives assistance to four hundred destitute families.)

- Provides a shelter for eighty elderly people.

- Community Outreach is accomplished on-site through a radio station, TV channel, video production studio, and offices to produce their monthly newspaper, "O Semeador" (the Sower of Seeds), a library and areas for art expositions.

- One lecture hall is capable of seating two thousand people. (It is sometimes used by musicians for concerts, and lecturers who speak to diverse topics.)

Founded in 1890, FEESP continues its Spiritist mission, applying its resources to the contemporary world. When I visited the last time, October, 2003, I was ushered around FEESP's fourteen story building by Leila Speeden, who is a hospital admistrator by day and a teacher at FEESP at night. She proudly told me, "FEESP has a 95% success rate with helping addicts to full recovery and helping suicidal people regain their emotional balance."

Help for the Addict

Leila described the process: "A person first enters into the basement area directly off the street. This is the "Department of Orientation and Direction." After he is interviewed to determine the type of assistance needed, he goes into an assembly room, where he listens to a talk. Typically the talk focuses on some teachings from the New Testament, explained in the light of principles of Spiritism. People who come here are already willing to re-evaluate their lives to some degree. The talk is to support that re-evaluation process and initiate the purification so necessary to inner transformation.

Most of the people coming in here have been motivated by intense emotion, even obsession and addiction. They have been leading relatively selfish lives, concerned with their own survival interests, more than the well-being of other people. The talks help them to stand back from their normal behavior, and see what they have caused by their own choices. It is not a complicated lesson to see: if you steal from others, they will steal from you. If you treat others poorly, others will, in turn, be unkind to you. *We help the people become more rational. The more rational we become, the more we see the necessity for spiritual and psychological transformation, and the more we can exert our will to make changes in the way we lead our lives.*"

After a person at FEESP hears the talk, he is ready to have a healing session. His mind is more focused, and his heart more open. He then waits his turn in a waiting area, before being called in for his session. Two to five trained mediums perform the energy passes, first for dis-obsession, then for treatment. The whole process lasts approximately five to ten minutes."

I asked Leila, "How are energy passes different than Reiki treatments (a Japanese form of spiritual healing)?" She replied, "Our mediums have the intention to bridge the person getting the healing with developed spirits who can help them. Reiki, on the other hand, is a direct transfer of energy from the healer, guided by God, to the person getting the healing."

Leila continued, "After eight weeks, the person sees an interviewer for the second time, to review his progress and determine his next steps.

After they receive the healing energy passes, most people stay on to take classes. At FEESP there are nine different levels of classes. They range in content from the "Basic Introduction to Kardec and his reflections on the New Testament," to advanced courses reserved for highly developed mediums. There are two tracks of study after the Basic courses. One is more intellectual study of the "Gospel" (as Explained by Spiritist Doctrine), the other is more practical learning to manage one's skills as a medium. Teachers meet with each individual students to decide on the track most well suited to them, after the basic course is complete."

Leila went on to describe more about what happens in the classrooms. The teacher is leading discussion and giving information. Dialogue with the students about what they believe is done in the spirit of increasing self-awareness, not being judgmental, or inspiring fear of retribution. Class sessions focus on clarifying moral guidelines from Kardec's books and also respecting free will of the students. The classes consider the advantages of following a path of spiritual growth, and the disadvantages of continuing in a way of life that indulges self-centered behaviors. Ultimately, Kardec's message is confrontive: Following the principles for spiritual evolution to what Kardec refers to as "perfection," brings happiness; selfishness breeds unhappiness. This ultimately demands that each student come to terms with the questions, "Which do I prefer? Am I willing to make a commitment? Am I willing to change my life?"

In this environment, Spiritists observe that addicts find direction, belong to a loving community, receive help releasing the disincarnates who possess them or cause them to obsess, and receive support for spiritual evolution. Spiritists believe that as people strengthen their commitment to spiritual principles, it becomes increasingly more difficult for intruding negatively motivated disincarnates to have any impact. These entities can only attach to people who have a weakness, a vulnerable spot, paralleling their own negativity. Someone with a tendency to anger attracts an entity who is intent on expressing anger. When that person has learned to rise above such a harmful emotion and control his anger, the entity can no longer attach himself to him/her. The power of entities, and their impact on psychological health, is recognized by some pioneering psychologists, e.g. Winafred Lucas, PhD., and psychiatrists, e.g. Arthur Guirdam, MD.

Elsie: Becoming a Leader

Elsie Dubugras, first mentioned in Chapter Two, took all the courses given through FEESP over a period of fourteen years, in the 40s and 50s. She also helped with the development of their School for Mediumship. After coursework, developing herself as a medium and healer, she left the safety of the center's walls, and worked with addicts, the mentally retarded and the suicidally depressed. She did what she could to help those who were suffering, wherever they were located. Within the group of advanced mediums, educated at FEESP, she was acknowledged as one of the "Fraternity of the Disciples of Jesus," for her dedication to helping others. Her loyalty to the Spiritist path was extraordinary in many ways, not the least of which was her pursuit of Spiritism during the time of military rule in Brazil (1945-1988) when governmental officials wanted the general public to consider it a crime to practice Spiritism.

She initially looked into Spiritism because she wanted to help her husband who had problems with addiction and depression, and was unable to support the family. "Unfortunately," she said, "I was not able to help him, because he didn't want help." Eventually, he committed suicide, leaving me to raise our two children. Elsie's way of dealing with the trauma of her husband's early death was to commit herself more deeply to her Spiritist activities.

Elsie had been working for Pan Am, using her skills as a medium to help them find people who were not paying their debts to the company. To do her work, Pan Am had paid her passage around the world a total of five times. Coming from an English mother and Danish father, Elsie has spent most of her life in Brazil. She speaks English, Portuguese and French fluently. After her husband's death, Elsie became an editor and translator for a magazine in Brazil focused on Parapsychology and Alternative Medicine.

In sum, it seems all Kardecist Centers are places where people help each other through compassion and a desire to build a human community based on wisdom and brotherhood. From 1920 to 1948, a highly evolved Master, DK, called the Tibetan, encouraged progress toward Brotherhood by writing through Alice Bailey, his channel, what life would be like when human beings are more capable of loving each other. FEESP is a reflection of what he wrote about:

"... it will be emphasized that all human beings are mani-festations of small fractions of the Spiritual One, who have taken on physical form to gain experience on Earth. These experiences are apparently essential for eventual achievement of spiritual perfection. It should therefore be realized that all human beings are closely related brothers, but brothers in different outer garb, and each and every one finding himself at his own particular stage of development on the difficult Path stretching before all. It will be stressed that life on Earth could be turned into something so much more beautiful, pleasant and bearable to all, if each individual would only con-tribute his small part towards sharing the amenities of life, showing greater tolerance and consideration in so many possible respects, and a greater display of love and goodwill in daily associations and interrelations.

The world is at present being flooded by these new and potent energies, and although the results are still somewhat obscured by the effects of well established older influences, such as selfish desire, greed, and hate, the reactions resulting from the ever spreading and deeper penetrating energies of universal love and good-will, are becoming noticeable, and these must and will eventually gain the upper hand, dominating all human relationships."

PART THREE

Building Blocks of Successful Kardecist Spiritist Centers

In order to create a Spiritist Center outside Brazil, you will need a viable structure for financial management, a curriculum for classes, a plan for the preparation of teachers responsible for teaching those classes, and a qualified advisor in charge of maintaining the quality of the spiritual healing and the teaching. Having the financial resources to attend the poor and the human resources to adequately train teachers, mediums and healers, is the backbone of any Kardecist Center.

It may be easier to start and maintain Spiritist Centers in Brazil, where the cost of living and real estate are considerably lower than the USA and other "first-world" countries. As I complete this book (February, 2004), Nancy Pelosi, Democratic Leader of the US House of Representatives, portrays the economic situation in the US this way: "the USA has a deficit of over four hundred billion dollars, hundreds of thousands of workers have been hit by the slumping economy, the cost of living continues to rise, and three million private sector jobs have been lost since the year 2000. The same day the US House of Representatives voted to support our troops in Iraq, it simultaneously voted to slash $28.3 billion for veterans' benefits and health care (reducing the size of social programs that feed hungry children and shield seniors from crippling medical bills)."

Many would say that starting a Spiritist Center which functions as a free service, and relies wholly on donations, may be unrealistic in this economic environment. This is to say nothing of the fact that the USA is not familiar with, and/or skeptical about, the philosophical foundations of Kardecismo. Where would one find teachers and mentors to conduct the schools? On the other hand, we have some business tycoons, like Bill Gates of Microsoft, who made billions when computer technologies were first gaining popularity, and they are now committing some of their wealth to the development of social programs for those who need special health care. Fifty-five percent of our population now consult alternative and complementary health care practitioners, usually spending out-of-pocket money as medical insurance does not cover these practitioners, for the most part. Some of our most well educated researchers are documenting scientific data that validate mediumship.[1] Even though starting a center seems challenging from an economic perspective, it may be founded because research, or a wealthy donor, has come to understand its value.

If it is not possible to start a Spiritist Center, we can consider importing components of Spiritist Centers, and implementing them in already existing Community Health Centers, clinics and hospitals. Parts of Kardec's philosophy, ideas about how to combine spiritual healing with study, and some of the activities one finds at Spiritist Centers—can be integrated.

Note: Centers that resemble, (or utilize components of Kardecist Spiritist Centers), do not need to be called "Spiritist." They may be called "Christian" or "Spiritual Healing Centers" or "Sanctuaries," or any other title that is suitable for the community in which they are located. "Kardecist Spiritist Center" has been solely used in this text to reference the centers in Brazil. A center that recognizes the existence of spirits, the Law of Karma and reincarnation, refers to Kardec's works and/or trains mediums certainly does not make it *exclusive* to "Spiritism." The principles from Kardecist Centers are free for anyone to use, as is the structure. There is no commercial trademark.

Please remember, however, there is strength in aligning with other Spiritist Centers that are anchored in the way of life put forth by Kardec and Chico Xavier. Also, having a singular philosophical anchor can strengthen the focus so necessary for the best kind of cooperative healing and mediumship. Even though they were written one hundred and fifty years ago, Kardec's writings are still very relevant today. They reflect universal and timeless truths.

Chapter Nine

Financial and Human Resources

The Organizational Structure

The following organizational structure comes from "Centro," one of one hundred Kardecist Centers in San Paulo. It is a bare-bones outline. Details of the anatomy of how the organization functions day-to-day are uniquely involved with the diverse needs of people in the community who come and go. How one Center applies this structure may well not be relevant for another Center.

At the top is the General Assembly, a group made up of those who want to assist in the management of the center. The assembly functions democratically, each person has a single vote. After making decisions, the Assembly directs "the Planning Council," (consisting of one person at Centro). This planner gives direction to the individual who is the "Fiscal Council" (who executes financial decisions), as well as to the "Executive Director." The Executive Director oversees the Center's programs in social assistance and educational classes, which are under the direction of two administrators: the Director of Social Assistance and the Director of Philosophical Classes. When necessary, the Executive Director consults with a specialist in Human Resources who can facilitate the effectiveness of the daily operating of the Center. Bookkeeping is managed by an administrative secretary who reports to the Executive Director.

There are seven divisions that report to the Director of Social Assistance, each with its own program leader: Walk-in Clinic, Courses for Pregnant Women, Legal Assistance, Sewing Workshop, Food, Social Assistance, and overseeing the needs of Alcoholics Anonymous/ Al-Anon (in its use of a room for its meetings at the Center). There are three leaders under the Director of Philosophical Classes: one for Spiritual Assistance (that includes energy passes and automatic writing), one for all Classroom Activities, and the other for Orientation to the center for first time visitors.

Managing Financial Resources

Raising Money

Spiritist Centers are not-for-profit organizations. Where does Centro get the money they need to function with each month, approximately USD $8,500? Only a small fraction comes from sales at the bookstore, café, and bazaar. The rest comes from donations from individuals and non-partisan groups.

The process of receiving donations is well organized. This is reassuring to donors who want know that money donated is received by a legally formed organization with "non-profit" status. Donors then reap the benefits of making a donation that is tax-deductible. Donors also receive receipts for donations, with acknowledgement of how the donation is being put to use, e.g. buying book supplies for a certain number of poor children, which allows them to attend school. This respectful communication and accountability between donors and the center's administration lubricates the flow of financial support of the community's functions. Donors are assured that their donations are not "lost" or mismanaged but are being of service to the community as a whole.

Centro manages to be debt-free and to expand. When I was last visiting, they were putting the finishing coat of paint on a four-story building for additional classrooms and assembly areas. They had continually been needing to find more space, acquiring adjacent buildings for meeting rooms almost every year, prior to the current new building. The Executive Director assured me they receive no contributions from any church or governmental agency. They are also unwilling to receive any contributions that have partisan "strings" attached. When a politician suggested he would donate a large sum of money to the Center, if they, in turn, allowed him to post promotional literature at the center endorsing his campaign, the donation was not accepted.

How can an organization proceed if no dependable funding agency is available? And, how does this happen in a "third-world" country like Brazil? A homeopathic physician who volunteers some time at Centro considered the question from the point of view of their philosophy. He said, "We find that if we place our faith in God, and continually practice alignment with the guidance we receive, we are never in debt. Something always happens to give us the support we need, without our having to compromise our integrity in any way. The supplier of our medications always gives us a thirty percent discount. Others simply donate supplies without any charge whatsoever. Grocery stores also give free donations of food. Individuals are generous."

Would this happen in the USA? Would it happen in other so-called "first world" countries? Who knows? But, the continued financial stability of Centro is certainly a testament to the generosity and charity of the Brazilian people. It may be that the only way to get a Spiritist Center started and functioning in a "first world" country, new to such Centers, would be through a large donation from a private individual, an "angel." If the Center proved to be of value to those who used its resources, then, it might be able to sustain itself through their donations. A Spiritist would say, "If God wants a Spiritist Center to be founded in a certain place, then the resources for the center will be there." (This offers no comfort to the pragmatists among us.)

Curiously, Centro has *never* functioned in the red, nor carried along debts from month to month. Do they enforce that dues be paid, or an initiation fee be expected from people when they first arrive? How do they ask people participating at the Center for financial support? The Executive Director said, "We never ask people for donations when they first come here. We don't have any donation boxes, nor signs asking for money. We want people to know that they can simply receive our full support without having to give anything in return. For some people, used to bargaining and strategizing to get what they want, coming to Centro is their first experience of human generosity."

"We find that when a person has received the support he/she needs, he/she then *wants* to give something back to the center. He/she then comes to my office with a donation." Similarly, the homeopathic physician added, "When we don't ask outright for donations it increases our faith as well as our certainty in God's intervention to help us and our mission."

Many of Brazil's Spiritist Centers manage to find the financial support they need in ways that seem impossible to us who live in a different culture. Traveling in Brazil one has to wonder, how would it change our experience of life in North America if we freely gave away what has been freely given to us? If we gave more generously and increased our faith, in keeping with what is written on our dollars, "In God We Trust," perhaps more of our essential needs would be answered.

One might think, with this unusually open and trusting attitude, which some will call "pie in the sky," no records would be kept. On the contrary, the Executive Administration keeps excellent records on every aspect of maintaining the building and services. They are not only accountable, paying bills in a timely way, but keep records so that summaries can be made quickly, assessing how many people are being served, in what ways. This, of course, facilitates the process of planning for the future—they can predict what needs they will have based on what resources visitors are currently using. This is especially important with regards to the pharmacy on site, as stocking the shelves and keeping them stocked depends on knowing what medications are being used most often (medication for hypertension was in highest demand. The next most needed medication was for controlling diabetes).

Allocating Money for Expenditures

Part of Centro's success in managing its funds is their acknowledging their priorities and their limitations, and applying this to the way they allocate money for expenditures. Centro chooses to apply all of their energy to helping the poor. A modest amount of money goes to the paid staff each month for janitorial services, kitchen staff for the café, a part-time licensed social worker who oversees the interviewers, and one administrative secretary who is also the bookkeeper.

Even though Centro has identified its first priority, it still must stay within the limits of its budget. For example, they limit how many packages of free food they can afford to give each month, based on prior months' donations. This prepares Centro's social assistants to recommend to some first-time visitors that they proceed immediately to other Spiritist Centers who may be able to help them, when Centro has reached its limit.

In the same vein, Centro asked me not to identify them in this book. They do not have the resources to receive international visitors. The treatment rooms are not large enough to hold people who come to observe. The halls are full with those waiting for treatments or interviews and not large enough to accommodate visitors. There is no one on staff who has the time to be a proper guide or translate for non-Portuguese speaking visitors. Time, money, staff, and space are at a premium.

In a similar vein, Centro has to make choices about the value of spending money for outreach. Kardec recommends that Spiritists share what Spiritism is about with anyone who is searching for spiritual evolution. It seems then, that money should be allocated for letting others know about the resources that can be found at a place such as Centro. In large cities in the USA, there is always space on buses and subways advertising various organizations that can give social assistance. Centro decided to let word of mouth be its spokesman, and allocates no money for outreach. This gives them the freedom to use all the money they have to help the poor.

No money is allocated for "clinical trials," to prove the effectiveness of energy passes for curing those who are ill. "Why prove it works by publishing our successes in a form that can be printed by a medical association," the Administration told me, "when the success of the work speaks for itself? We don't want to prove anything to anyone, nor do we care to confront or create opposition with medical authorities. When the time is right for medicine to see the value in what we do, they will come to us. Before that time, we will continue doing what we can to help the poor. That is our job."

Anyone building a Kardecist Center will have to make choices such as these, and determine what their priorities are to be.

Chapter Ten

Classes and the Preparation of Teachers

H ow does a school for training mediums and healers manage to function side-by-side with a social service organization dedicated to helping the poor with food, medical help, legal advice, and classes on principles to live by? Think of it as a "one-room school house," where students of all ages and stages of personal evolution work together, helping each other gain more understanding and skills. Even the teachers are in this "fish-bowl" environment, watching each other, offering each other both constructive criticism and help, insuring certain standards are maintained. In this way, each individual grows in his/her unique way at his/her own pace, with many different opportunities for learning and diverse teachers to learn from.

Although North Americans are familiar with the one-room schoolhouse model, they find a Kardecist educational center outside their frame of reference. Wouldn't the subtle spiritual work of the mediums be impossible next to the rough world of the street people? How could you expect an inexperienced medium, beginning to learn how to communicate with invisible disincarnate beings, to concentrate, when faced with hallways full of indigent young pregnant teenagers worried about their physical survival, a toddler whining at their feet. It would seem more efficient to have separate buildings: a School for Mediumship in one, and welfare services in another.

In Brazilian Kardecist Spiritist Centers, the two are actually inseparable. The mediums and teachers are improving their skills as they work with those coming for assistance. Those needing help need the free services of the mediums and teachers. The presence of those in need is a steady reminder to the mediums that their intention is to be of service, not to make their pursuit of psychic phenomena a self-serving path of personal aggrandizement. The street people look at the healers, mediums, and teachers as role-models, and feel uplifted by their presence, as they are reminders that feeling at peace is possible.

Following is information about the content of the Basic courses, training for mediumship, becoming a healer, and/or teacher. If you review the stages of evolution outlined in the chapter "Personal Spiritual Evolution," you will see that the classes are stepping stones advancing growth through those Levels. Of course, the sequence of evolution is never a step by step process, like graduating through successive classes, as each individual is at various levels of personal spiritual evolution in each domain of life.

The Basic Course

As mentioned earlier in the text, every person taking part in the activities of the Center is required to attend the Basic Course.

The Basic Course meets for two hours, once a week for thirty weeks. Each class begins with an initial prayer. One hour and ten minutes is spent studying the principles of life presented in "The Spirits' Book;" forty minutes is spent on the study of the "Gospel as Explained by Spiritist Doctrine." Within the first eight weeks, students have been introduced to the philosophical, scientific and religious aspects of Spiritism; evidence of the existence of God, properties of the material world vis-a-vis the spiritual world. They have looked at the difference between intelligence and instinct, and acknowledged the possibility of the existence of the "peri-spirit," the semi-material aspect of spirit, or spiritual energy, that inhabits the body and leaves the body at death. Students have studied the progression of spiritual evolution and learned how to discern evolved spirits from less developed spirits, evolved people from less developed people. Most importantly, they have studied the goals of incarnation, of the soul and the reason for life in a physical body.

Continuing on, they are presented with information about what happens in life after death when the soul separates from the body. By the tenth week they are considering reincarnation and progressive evolution through lifetimes. By the fourteenth week they study how a spirit prepares for its next incarnation, bringing its moral and intellectual development with it from previous lifetimes. After four months the students are considering how spirits interact with those in body, by influencing their thoughts. Finally, a study of the Divine and Natural Laws of Life, leads the student to what must be accomplished before the goal of "Perfection" is achieved. Developing ethical and moral behavior is essential. All of the topics above are succinctly addressed in the "The Spirits'."

The Goal of the Basic Course

The Basic Course begins to awaken the mind, to explain to the common man practical ways of making life choices. It helps people begin the process of self-reflection. Throughout the Basic Course students discuss principles of living that lead to evolution and those that lead to an erosion of personal power. Inevitably, the very study of these books guides the students into making choices as to what they want to believe, and how they want to conduct their lives in the future.

Study of texts and self-awareness go hand in hand. Students begin to increase their self-awareness by studying their own actions and responses to others, relative to the lessons presented in the class reading. Students develop their ability to observe and choose their behaviors, rather than react automatically or emotionally without thinking. They also discuss the results of actions over time: "What will be the quality of life if I continue to be unkind to others? What will be the quality of life if I learn to be kind to myself and others? What does life look like when people are consistently kind and respectful to each other?"

Students are consistently brought to reflect on how Kardec's teachings have been relevant over time, and applicable to diverse people because *The Spirit's Book* and the *Gospel* are presented in the context of current events, and current research, as well as other philosophers (e.g. Socrates and Plato). Science and philosophy are woven together to demonstrate Natural Laws, especially cause and effect, and their interaction with God's Laws. For instance, good will leads to cooperative ventures that bring social and financial success. One can trust in Divine Justice, i.e. natural law will bring negative effects to those who have selfish motivation. Therefore, it may be more appropriate for people to learn from each other, rather than take on roles of punishing each other.

> The uneven distribution of happiness and misery on Earth—between well-meaning and ill-meaning people—can be explained only in the context of many lifetimes, and only if we accept Earth's current state as a place of expiation. Inequities exist in appearance alone. Our trouble is that for the most part we see them entirely from the point of view of the present. Once we broaden our perspective—to the point where we can see the succession of lives—we realize that every person is given just what he or she needs to experience (that is, after taking into account progress made in the spirit world). Then it becomes clear that God's Justice is unvarying.
>
> — *The Gospel Explained by Spiritist Doctrine*

The collective wisdom of highly evolved spirits, in Kardec's works, helps students understand the destiny that awaits us in our return to the spirit world at death. Those at all levels of consciousness, feel comforted, as the message is one of assistance and forgiveness. Students come to understand that on entering the future life they will first be judged by their humility, selflessness, benevolence, charity and compassion, but also given the assistance they need, at every step of the path, to continue on their path of evolution.

As one accepts the view Kardec recorded about death and the after life, one comes to understand how to lead his/her life in this world in a way that brings inner peace of mind both in this realm and in the future realm, as spirits. The core message transcends time and religious form. It emphasizes,

> "If you have love, you have the most precious thing on Earth."
>
> — *The Gospel Explained by Spiritist Doctrine*

Kardec's message is the revelation of highly evolved spirits; it fits with the essence of every religion; it is a path of love. Some Christians who regard Kardec as a re-conceptualization of Christianity, find his teachings clarify what is vague, and put forth a more consistently compassionate interpretation of Biblical teachings. There is no mention of "an eye for an eye, and a tooth for a tooth." Forgiveness is embraced, as opposed to retribution. The belief in reincarnation, which may have been removed from the Bible in the 6th century (see Appendix One for more details), brings consolation that we will again see those we have been close to, when we meet them in subsequent lives. Kardec tells us one can develop one's own direct relationship to God and highly evolved spirits. One doesn't need a priest to mediate, but one must take responsibility for the fact that spirits surround us and we must decide what kind of spirits we are willing to listen to: highly evolved, less-evolved or misguided, negatively motivated spirits.

> "The Spirit world is presented not as a supernatural element but as one of the living and active forces of Nature, the source of a vast number of phenomena that even today we don't understand and so relegate to the realm of fantasy or miracles."
>
> — *The Gospel Explained by Spiritist Doctrine*

Introducing Kardecist Spiritism to Children

When one looks through the resources of the FEESP bookstore in downtown San Paulo one finds many books for young people introducing the same ideas presented in the Basic Course: the Law of Karma, seeing life as a process of evolution of consciousness, the nature of disincarnates, reflections on the existence of beneficent spirits who help us, and negatively motivated disincarnate spirits who can obstruct us. These books for six to twelve-year-olds also impart basic personal skills needed to avoid the impact of negative spirits— often in an entertaining and colorful way. A child can understand just as well as an adult: the antidote to being affected by negative spirits is to attract positive spirits through loving action, charity and good will. (One would find this information in the United States only in esoteric schools for adults studying paranormal phenomena.)

> "We need to resist the suggestions of misguided spirits who, by their wicked thoughts, try to turn us away from the path of goodness."
>
> — *The Gospel Explained by Spiritist Doctrine*

Labwork and Pre-requisites for the Basic Course

When students are not in class, they can be involved in other Spiritist activities that build on the classroom study—let's call it the "Labwork." When a student of the Basic Course receives Energy passes he/she is receiving the felt sense of his/her own subtle energy body. The possibility that the peri-spirit exists, also becomes more real to the student, as mediums are treating them "as if" they are an immortal spirit temporarily housed in a physical body. The loving attention and energy transmission by healers effects healing, and strengthens the bonds of community. Automatic writing gives them the notion that loved ones who have passed on are available, and can be contacted. This builds further on the sense of community and meaningful connection on a human level, but also connecting with spirits.

The Soup Kitchen can be the most important step in the direction of learning. No one is expected to attend a lecture or a class until his/her belly is full. A bowl of soup and a piece of bread are sometimes vital to a student's ability to concentrate in class. The poor are also assured that they will have sufficient food for their survival, once they are under the care of the Center. This also frees them to focus on their emotional and mental response to life, beyond their immediate physical needs.

Sign at Centro, posted in several meeting rooms in prominent places:
"Fraternity is everything."

After the Basic Course: Further Study

After the Basic Course, students can proceed to a deeper study of *The Gospel As Explained by Spiritist Doctrine*. This classroom experience is further encouragement to align with moral principles of life, illustrated in the parables of the New Testament.

After a certain amount of course study in the Gospel (different in each center), each student decides with his/her teacher if it is appropriate to develop mediumship and healing, or continue to study the Gospel.

Students are not advised to go on to specific classes in the study of mediumship unless they are able to act in an ethical manner. A medium can only learn to use his/her paranormal power correctly if he/she has a strong foundation in ethical behavior. Until that foundation is in place, learning mediumship skills is not advised. Mediumship is not appropriate for those on a quest for power to be used for selfish gain, but only for those who want to help others in need of consolation, guidance and real help.

Teachers in Kardecist Centers therefore encourage students to study the Gospel until such time as they have transformed their motivation from acquiring personal power and ego-centered behaviors to the desire to be of service to others. Mediumship is not something to be sensationalized or commercialized. It is also not a choice made by the Ego (Mental or Emotional levels of consciousness). All the activities of a Spiritist Center, including mediumship, are a product of the activation and loyal discipline to moral and altruistic principles.

"Recall that every person on Earth has a mission, some greater than others; but whatever form it takes, it's always designed to further love in the world."
— *The Gospel Explained by Spiritist Doctrine*

Students can, and sometimes do, continue on with increasingly deeper levels of the study of the Gospel for a number of years. This is indispensable for further personal growth as well as preparation for training as a healer or medium. Increasing awareness of the impact of selfish behavior inevitably leads to a profound personal transformation.

In the Gospel of Matthew, 13, 1-9, one finds the parable of the Sower:

"A farmer went out to sow his seed. As he was scattering the seed, some fell along the path, and the birds came and ate it up. Some fell on rocky places, where it did not have much soil. It sprang up quickly, because the soil was shallow. But, when the sun came up, the plants were scorched, and they withered because they had no root. Other seed fell among thorns, which grew up and choked the plants. Still other seed fell on good soil, where it produced a crop—a hundred, sixty or thirty times what was sown. He who has ears, let him hear."

From *The Gospel Explained by Spiritist Doctrine*:

"The parable of the sower represents the various ways we can make use of gospel teachings...We can just apply the parable to the different kinds of Spiritists among us. In it we find symbolized the Spiritists who are primarily attracted by phenomena, who seek only to satisfy their curiosity, and who fail to learn anything of worth from them. The parable also brings to mind those Spiritists who find the brilliance of spirit communication interesting only as long as it satisfies their imaginations and who continue to be just as cold and indifferent as before. Then there are the ones who consider the spirits' advice very good and admirable but only supply it to others—never to themselves. Finally, we find in the parable those Spiritists for whom the teachings are like seeds that have fallen on good soil, and that produce fine fruit."

Training for Mediumship

"Mediumship is a mission, and should always be exercised as such."
— *The Mediums' Book*, by Allan Kardec

When a teacher in consultation with each individual student has determined that the student is ready for the coursework in mediumship, he/she takes a two-hour course, "Curso de Mediuns" (The Course for Mediums) for thirty weeks. This training can continue on, as is right for the individual, for a number of years. Following is a summary taken from the syllabus used at "Centro" for the first year, second year, and third years of mediumship training.

In the first year the student studies, in the following order: The make-up of the physical body with special attention to the nervous system and brain. The spiritual body, with special attention to the peri-spirit, and auras. The energy centers or chakras: their description, function, and relationship to physical nerve plexes (centers). Action of spirits on the material level.

Intervention of spirits in the physical world. The nature of mediumship with special attention to natural mediumship, Spiritist mediumship, the mediumship of Jesus Christ, receiving Grace, and mediumship with animals. Signs of mediumship with special attention to the sensations felt in the process of being a medium. The formation of a medium with special attention to the moral base of the person and the dissolution of mediumship when that moral base erodes. The theme of the moral obligations continues with special attention to how one can lose one's gifts as a medium if one reverts to immoral behavior. How to identify certain kinds of spirits. How to evoke spirits. How to direct questions to the spirits. Contradictions and confusions that may present themselves in the world of being a medium. Charlatanism and glamour (being a medium for the purpose of glorifying one's ego). The process of thinking with special attention paid to the conscious, subconscious and super-conscious mind, as well as habits of mind (e.g. vices such as jealousy, self-centeredness and gossiping). The importance of being vigilant with the mind, prayer, taking responsibility, and continual study of inspired teachings. Explanation of the activities of the Center.

The books used in the course of study above are: Kardec's *The Spirits' Book*, *Genesis*, and *the Mediums' Book*; *Mediumship* and *Passes and Radiations* by Edgard Armond, and channeled teachings from Chico Xavier: *the Source of Life*, *The Messengers*, *The World Above*, *The Path of Light*, *The Domain of Mediums*, *Missionaries of Light*, *Thoughts of Life*, and *Evolution in Two Worlds*. Thirty minutes of each class is devoted to studying "*The Messengers*" by Andre Luiz. Unfortunately, the only books in this list that have been translated into English are those by Kardec. However, Dr. Gary Schwartz, professor of psychology, medicine, neurology, and psychiatry at the University of Arizona, has an excellent list of more than fourteen recommended readings listed in the back of his book "The Afterlife Experiments: Breakthrough Scientific Evidence of Life After Death" (2002). Schwartz recommends both audiotapes and books under the heading of "The Science of Mediumship, After-Death Communications, and Parapsychology" and "The Art of Mediumship: Personal and Professional."

The classes at Centro are similar to formal academic classes one might find in a classroom with more ordinary subject matter. Just because the subject is esoteric, does not mean the classroom lacks discipline and rigor. The teacher of the course assigns each individual particular kinds of study to amplify the course work. Students are also expected to study other books during their two month-long vacations between classes.

In the second year, the following themes are studied in order: The relationship between thinking and mediumship. The origin of thought formation. The discernment of thinking, hypnosis and conditioned reflexes; telepathy, and Kirlian photography. The difference between animism and mediumship. Animistic phenomena. Inspiration and intuition with special attention to communication with nature. Classification of mediumship related to levels of consciousness. Classification of mediums who follow Kardec with special attention to how mediumship affects the body, physical senses, sleep-walking and healing. Special types of mediums. Partial and total incorporation of spirits. Automatic writing and automatic hearing, inspired poetry, music and art. Clairvoyance and clairaudience with special attention to distortions in time and space, spiritual and psychic seeing, including seeing apparitions and remote viewing. Psychometry. Dreams. Review of energy centers, or Chakras. Mediumship and Spiritual Healing. Energy passes with special attention to the mechanics and function of energy when doing passes. The will of the patient. Magnetic healing of a spiritual nature, with attention to the history and evolution of magnetism and its relationship to spirituality. Explanation of the activities of the Centro.

The main text for this course is "*The World Above*" by Andre Luiz, as channeled through Xavier. In addition to some of the books in the prior course there is "*Animism and Spiritism*" by Alexandre Aksakof, "*The Problem of Being, Destiny and Suffering*" by Frenchman, Leon Denis, and "*The Phenomenon of Spiritism*" by Gabriel Delanne. Hopefully these books will be translated into English in the near future.

Although the class proceeds with intellectual study and lectures, half the class is devoted to applying the skills of mediumship. I was told that only some schools of mediumship train students in the skills of incorporating a disincarnate. Centro does not. FEESP does.

Between the second and third year, each student reviews his/her commitment to the training with a teacher. The teacher makes it clear that moving forward in training will demand full participation on the level of body, mind and soul. This is not a training one can audit, or visit. This is a training that demands wholehearted commitment and deep personal transformation.

112

The third year of training is again a two-hour class, once a week, for thirty weeks. This year is a study of principles, with half an hour devoted to studying the book, *"Liberation"* by Andre Luiz channeled through Chico Xavier, and twenty-five minutes of practicum. Five minutes of prayer begin and end each class.

In the following order students study: Mediumship, its physical effects— physical phenomena like ectoplasm and psycho-kinesis. Physical effects are covered in more depth looking specifically at materialization, extraordinary paranormal phenomena, and forms of channeled speaking and writing. Poltergeist. Obsession. Mental fixations. Telepathy. Mental influences. Possession. Fascination. Dis-obsession. Spiritual reunion. Orientation to spiritual life and giving interviews, including role-playing to prepare for work at the center. Explanation of the activities of the Centro.

This ends the three year-long classes on mediumship, but there are also more advanced classes for mediums who choose to go on. These cover particular aspects of mediumship in more depth, according to the interests and needs of the students and teacher.

[The boy had followed an inner vision that took him to a vast, dry desert. Now he wasn't sure he could survive.] The Alchemist said to him:

"Remember what I told you: the world is only the visible aspect of God. And what alchemy does is to bring spiritual perfection into contact with the material plane..."

If I'm not able to turn myself into the wind, we're going to die," the boy said...

"You're the one who many die," the Alchemist said. "I already know how to turn myself into the wind."

—*The Alchemist* by Brazilian author, Paulo Coelho

Currently, in the USA, being a medium, a psychic, or a healer is considered irrational, even a mark of mental illness—or glamorous, e.g. TV personalities, like John Edwards, giving readings for movie stars during primetime make mediumship look very glamorous. People are either fascinated by mediums, or dismiss them as unreal, or frauds. Some fascinated by mediumship, aspire to cultivate those skills, in order to reap the glamorous life of being special in the public eye. Some of these same mediums charge high fees for "readings." They are loath to stop their work if it means no longer collecting fees for payment. So, if their gifts begin to weaken, these mediums may still continue to practice, but their readings no longer reflect the truth. In this environment, rarely is a medium perceived as fulfilling a mission or being in service to a spiritual goal, rarely are mediums considered as having something to offer religion, psychology or the sciences.

The glamour aspect of mediumship has no place in Spiritist Centers. Mediumship is a mission, and a way to be of service to others. It is not commercialized. The selflessness expected of the medium can be observed in many Spiritist leaders. Elsie Dubugras, who became a Disciple of Jesus after completing fourteen years of coursework in a Spiritist Center, and then practicum working amongst the suffering and dispossessed, said to me, "I am just a little ant." This woman is a linguist, an editor, a writer and researcher at the top of her field, but, in her humility described herself as an ant, merely doing her duty. More than once, when I said "thank you" or acknowledged her for a special gift, I heard her say, "You don't need to say thank you, I am only doing my duty."

Being a medium is
Not a privilege but an opportunity.
Not a grace, but a bridge
Not a talent, but an act of charity and forgiveness.

— Divaldo P. Franco

Mediums are expected to be honest, too. Elsie said, "A medium is an honest person who doesn't lie or invent things." Students are selected for mediumship training by their willingness to tell the truth about who they are and what they experience. That honesty and openness is a cornerstone. It is imperative for the training, as teachers and students often share constructive criticism, both informally, and at an annual formal review. This appraisal of mediumship skills prevents mediums/healers from working when they are not able to be fully honest. It also allows mediums/healers to be human, i.e., every person, no matter what their mission, has good and bad periods. Each one of us needs to be given the time to disengage from work and renew ourselves when we are out of balance. Having community support for this is a boon.

Training to Give Energy Passes

"The cell is a machine driven by energy. It can thus be approached by studying matter, or by studying energy. In every culture and in every medical tradition before ours, healing was accomplished by moving energy."

— Szent-Gyorgyi

Training for giving energy passes is given twice a year. The student does not need to have completed mediumship training to take this course. There are five classes in this training. The book that is studied is Armond's *"Passes and Radiations."* The real training occurs in the weeks and years that follow the training, as healers learn how to implement what they have learned in the classroom and by studying the book. They have to learn to trust their own way of working. Even though Armond specifies certain ways of doing energy passes to address certain problems, students at Centro, are encouraged to recognize their own guidance, and perfect their own gifts and their own style. Graduates of the course practice their skills giving energy passes to assist those coming for healing and cures.

Mediums and healers at Spiritist Centers often have to work hard. After classroom activity, they do a practicum under supervision that often lasts for years. On top of this, they are asked to cultivate personal qualities that may not only test their patience, but demand personal transformation of the highest degree. Because of excellent training, some Spiritist Centers in Brazil have superlative results in the healing they can offer. It seems it is time we acknowledge that successful Spiritist Centers are pioneering a way to a transformation in medicine, (perhaps even a revitalization of religion). This can be very instructive to those looking for positive options.

DK acknowledged the value of such healing when he wrote,

"When trained healers, with perception, with a full working knowledge of the etheric body, with an understanding of the energies which compose it and which it does or can transmit, of the subtle constitution of man and of the methods of directing energies from one point and location to another, can work with full medical knowledge or in full collaboration with the orthodox physician or surgeon then tremendous changes will be brought about. Great enlightenment will reach the race of men. It is for this that we must prepare—not primarily for the healing of the physical body, but because of the expansion of the consciousness of the race that this new and esoteric study will bring about."

— *Esoteric Healing*,
(Alice Bailey), 1953

Preparation of Teachers

Della, had been part of the community of Centro for fifteen years. She was introduced to Kardecist Spiritism there, and, having participated fully in all the coursework, was now teaching advanced classes in mediumship. Della commented on how Centro prepares teachers for classes. She said, "It seems to be a natural process. While a student is completing all of his/her coursework, he/she may recognize a natural inclination to teach the materials. The person may have a natural talent for teaching, as well as a desire to give to others. That student then confers with one or more teachers, expresses the desire to teach, and then gradually is encouraged to step into that role. I think it may be a soul agreement that a person makes for this lifetime. At a certain point, the person "remembers" the mission and then finds his/her way to teach.

There are no rigid criteria for becoming a teacher. Here, at Centro, the teachers watch the students matriculate through the various classes. It simply becomes apparent who will make a good teacher. One looks for compassion, integrity, a good understanding of the materials and skills, and, of course, a desire to teach others. When someone asks to teach, and other teachers honor his/her request, then several teachers meditate and pray about the request. In essence they ask the spirits aligned with the Center if this person is appropriate to prepare to become a teacher. If the spirits aligned with the Center are in accord with the decision the teachers and student have made, the student may then proceed to an internship.

The next step involves being a "Secretary" to a class. The Secretary is preparing to teach by being present at every scheduled class meeting, and acting as an assistant to the experienced teachers. There are always two teachers for each of the Basic classes, so the Secretary is the third person on the team. Since each person on the team has different aptitudes, the Director of Philosophical Classes makes the assignment as to which class teachers are assigned to and who the members of each teaching team will be.

Every three years the teachers must change the level of the class they teach. This stimulates the teachers to learn in depth about new areas. Ideally, students also continue to work with different teachers. It is understood that if a student is with the same teacher continually, he/she tends to perceive that person as an idol or a guru. This is *not* what the school wants to cultivate.

As the newest teacher gains confidence, he/she takes on more and more of the actual classroom presentation, gradually retiring one of the experienced members of the team. The Secretary takes on the role of teacher, partnering with a more experienced teacher, and supervising a new "Secretary." The teacher being retired from one team goes on to become part of a new team, with a new class. In this way, with regular changes each year, the community of teachers develop close relationships yet individuals maintain their ability to work with different kinds of people, constantly renewing their knowledge of the material from different levels of classes.

Similar to the mediums, the teachers are also subject to review. They are supportive of each other as each individual progresses at the pace of their spiritual evolution, and certain standards are expected. It is the responsibility of the Director of Philosophical Classes to assure that those who are teaching can model the qualities brought forth through the coursework: discipline, high moral standards, compassion, self-awareness, love and charity. Teachers are also expected to keep themselves up-to-date with general knowledge of physics, medicine, and the natural sciences.

The community of the Spiritist Center is attractive to many people for diverse reasons. The poor need help. Those who are natural mediums want to take command of their gifts in service of others. Some professionals want to volunteer their services. Others have a calling to be teachers, to help awaken others to their path of evolution. Each person fits into a unique spot in the community. If someone comes in, and wants to play a role, he/she is first asked to do odd jobs to become acquainted with the

Center activities and people, as well as take the Basic Course. Continuing on like this, at some point, each person sees where he/she fits in. That recognition is an organic process, unfolding between the administration and the new member, as well as whatever this new person and his/her own guidance. Of course, as people find their places, the bonds of the community grow increasingly stronger.

"Fraternity is Everything."

Martha Thomas adds to this: "We have to teach people to learn to work together, and not do everything alone."

Finding Teachers and Mentors Outside Brazil

Hopefully Martha's idea about working together will also span countries and cultures, as we need teachers and mentors capable of creating and maintaining schools for mediumship in other countries. How will we find these people? It is highly likely that the international exchange will continue to progress as the world gets "smaller"— Brazilian teachers well-schooled in mediumship in Brazil, will come to the United States to share their knowledge and skills, and more North Americans will learn Portuguese so they can attend classes in Brazil. I hope this book contributes to the building of that bridge.

Of course, a stepping stone to further integration of Kardec's philosophy is that teachers and mentors schooled in the United States bring the study of Kardec (*The Spirits' Book*, *The Mediums' Book*, *The Gospel Explained by Spiritist Doctrine*) into the classes they teach here, combining them with study materials developed in the USA (see Suggested Reading).

Chapter Eleven

First Steps Toward Creating A Center in Your Town

This chapter provides general recommendations on first steps in beginning to form a Spiritist Center. It outlines legislation that has created parameters around the practice of healers at Brazil's Spiritist centers, and also relates how the laws for pastoral counseling in the USA allow spiritual healing, similar to energy passes. A brief profile of the five models of Spiritist centers described earlier in the book—along with a few general parameters— is located at the end of the chapter, to facilitate your discussion of how you can import components to enhance existing centers, or create a center in your town.

Fraternity and Fraternities

What is needed when starting a Spiritist Center is the same as what is needed in maintaining a Spiritist Center, "Fraternity is everything." Centro didn't start until 1977, twenty years after one family member initially was motivated to begin. Why? When she asked the spirits for guidance, she received the reply, "Take twenty years for the whole family to work together as volunteers at an existing Spiritist Center. Continue your classroom studies. This will develop fraternity amongst everyone in the family. When you have this, you will be prepared to set up and successfully manage your own center."

Is it essential for everyone to persevere through twenty years of study and community work to be adequately prepared? No. But, it is necessary to create a strong bond among the people who will maintain the center and teach the classes. Managing successful Spiritist Centers is a cooperative effort. There are various ways to create that strong bond.

In Brazil, I heard it more than once from various mediums working at different Centers: Oftentimes the people drawn together to start a Center have spent other lives together as friends and/or family. They may not recognize it in their very first meetings, but it emerges that they are part of a particular fraternity of souls. These kinds of fraternities sometimes decide to incarnate together to perform a certain function, or accomplish a specific goal. This does not necessarily mean that the Center they manage will run perfectly smoothly. On the contrary, it may mean that the group has work to do before they can work together. They must learn to let go of past conflicts and regrets, and let go of conflicts that may emerge as they work together in this lifetime. Sorting out the past, and re-orienting to the present can take time. Also, each member of the team needs to progress to a level of consciousness in which he/she has the inner resources to cooperate with others. This does not come easily to everyone.

It is also necessary for the human team who maintains the Center to maintain a strong bond with the fraternity of spirits who are watching over the center, their "Spiritual Fraternity." Martha Thomaz recounted the origins of the Federation of Brazilian Spiritists in San Paulo, FEESP, the largest satellite of FEB, described in Chapter Eight:

"The FEESP was initiated by a strong spiritual fraternity of disincarnates, called the "Four Leaf Clover. " This fraternity concentrated their efforts in Brazil to help re-orient and educate Brazilians after World War II. This fraternity guided Commander Armond when he met with the initial group of mediums who developed the School for Mediumship as part of the FEESP, and helped him organize and train these mediums as the "Fraternity of the Disciples of Jesus."

For ten years the Fraternity of the Four Leaf Clover stayed very close to the FEESP in order to guide its development. Since the mediums organizing the School were very well developed, it initially took only twenty minutes for them to receive guidance from the spiritual fraternity to start the School. When the School was functioning, and the details of the curriculum for all four years of coursework was in place, the fraternity retreated. Their initial work was complete. Now it was time for the human fraternity to strengthen their confidence so they could manage the School, rather than rely only on the voice of those in the spiritual fraternity."

The concept of an organization of social welfare and spiritual evolution existing side by side was a new phenomena for me—now, recognizing that the institution had been guided by disincarnate spirit guides was yet another step. Despite the radical nature of what I was hearing (my mind was challenged to accept it), I asked Martha to describe more to me about the fraternities. I was wondering, "Does every Spiritist Center have a spiritual fraternity who guides them?"

Martha continued, "There are independent fraternities in each country and each fraternity is drawn to doing a unique kind of spiritual work to support the evolution of human kind. They each have a different strategy. The nature of each of the fraternities I am most aware of is written in the book I just published, *"Bringing Together the Fraternities of the Universe with the Fraternities of Space"* (not yet translated into English). A number of different disincarnate spirits collaborated with me as I wrote. We were most interested in describing the existence of various spiritual fraternities who are responsible for evolution on this planet."

First Steps in the USA

Since I am interested in the possibility of Spiritist centers being set up in the USA, I asked, "Is there a fraternity watching over the USA which would help in setting up a center there?"

She answered: "You don't need to start by contacting a fraternity. There are three steps: First, get together with a few friends of like mind. Cultivate your connection together. Discuss your mutual interests. Meditate and pray together. Offer love to the spiritual plane [by expressing appreciation and gratitude]. Ask for help in making life on this planet better.

Soon one or more of you will begin to get a sense of clarity about your next steps as a group. Watch to see what special talents are revealed in the group. The resources you share amongst you will guide the development of your specific Center. Cooperate to manifest the development of the Center, using the resources you have. In this way, your human fraternity will unfold organically over time and find the form for the organization that you want to create. It may or may not look like Centro, or any other Brazilian Spiritist Center.

Be methodical. Get together once a week at the same time of day, or for a whole day. Look at the real needs of your specific community. Be sure that as you create your center you are addressing those real needs. Also reflect the cultural values of your area. Don't try to force people to accept something they don't value. At the same time, offer what is in line with the resources you have. Do not offer what you cannot provide. The gifts of each of the members of your group will show you what you can give. You will have gifts and limitations. Be clear as to what those limitations are, just as you are clear on what your gifts are. Then, teach people not to do everything alone. It's important to create friends. Learn to work together."

She was reassuring, "You don't have to take twenty years to create a fraternity to work together. In time, as your vibrations as individuals and as a group become more refined and close-knit, you will attract others of like mind. More mediums will join you. I'll tell you what the spirits told us when we were starting the School for Mediumship for FEESP. This would be your second step:

Study *The Gospel — Explained by Spiritist Doctrine* together. Then, work on your own vibrations. The higher your state of consciousness, the more you have perfected your own body and mind to be pure of heart, the higher your energy vibrations will be.

Your third step is to work with a mentor. (Commander Armond was our mentor in those early years. We had to be willing to have him instruct us, and follow his instructions.) It was made very clear that we should stick to Kardecist Spiritism as our philosophical anchor, and try not to bring other philosophies into the school that might confuse or diffuse the student mediums' attention.

Appeal to the fraternities for help by using the prayer of the spiritual fraternities. Then they will make themselves available to your mission."

Prayer of the Fraternities

Our Divine Master and Savior
Strengthen us and support us
So that we can fight against
the Forces of Evil that
Try to dominate our World.

Venerable celestial messengers,
assistants of Jesus,
Strengthen us and support us
So that we can fight against
the Forces of Evil that
Try to dominate our World.

Our Father, our Creator,
Eternal source of love and light,
Strengthen us and support us
So that we can fight against
the Forces of Evil that
Try to dominate our World.

Personal Note

After I had the opportunity to watch mediums at work in healing and automatic writing at Centro, I went to interview Martha Thomaz, the trusted mentor to the mediums and healers. Martha had just completed writing a book on fraternities, and gave me a copy. I was both fascinated by, and skeptical of the idea of invisible leagues of highly evolved spirits willing to lend us a hand.

Martha looked at me with a kind but penetrating gaze. I sensed her looking into the invisible energy around me, gleaning information on another level. She told me, "You have a connection to the 'Fraternity of the Liberators' in North America. This includes Abraham Lincoln, Thomas Edison, and Thomas Paine as well as many North American Indians. They are here with you, learning about Brazilian Spiritism with you. They can also help you when you get back to North America and are continuing your work."

My translator, Julika Kiskos, teased me later, "You mean I've had all those people in my car at once? I'll have to charge you extra!"

Actually Martha encouraged me to start a Spiritist Center in the USA. Elsie had done the same when I interviewed her a few days earlier. Excited by their encouragement, and in awe of the door they were opening in front of me, I told them, "I would rather first describe a blueprint of a Spiritist Center in writing for others so that many Centers can be developed all over the world. I feel this is what I am now called to do."

I needed time to contemplate what role I wanted to play. At the back of my mind I wondered, "Would I have a hand in managing a specific center?" At this point, I realize, "Yes, I can help start a center...I can help others start centers, or consult with those implementing components of Spiritist Centers." This is currently beginning to happen, as more people go to Brazil from the US and spend time at the Kardecist Centers.

Restrictions and Successes

A volunteer at Centro once said in an interview, "Difficulties will inevitably arise. But, they can be a necessary element to help make you more strong and clear in your direction. It is through our troubles that we reach out to new people, make new connections, and open ourselves to new perspectives. Just because we suffer with problems does not mean we have karma that needs to be atoned for. Instead, problems offer a doorway to new knowledge—even a new kind of culture, and a new time."

One of the areas that everyone involved with healing must attend to is the law. No one can legally diagnose and offer treatment of disease without a medical license. Currently, psychologists and psychotherapists are not allowed to touch clients (this is to insure that no inappropriate sexual contact is made.) Certified massage practitioners and physicians are licensed to touch clients. Pastoral Counselors, by definition, attend to the spiritual needs of their clients. They can offer spiritual healing. In the USA, we don't have licensing, only certification programs that endorse trained spiritual healers to share what they know. Of course, we *do* have laws protecting us against paraprofessional health practitioners who make fraudulent claims.

We also have FDA regulations, combined with American Medical Association restrictions, which have severely limited the use of Energy

Medicine protocols. The FDA, as Dan Haley reports,[1] controls more than it was originally mandated to do in 1906. It was supposed to make sure foods were pure and drugs were safe. It now claims regulatory authority over drugs, but defines a drug as anything that is used to diagnose or treat disease. This applies to electromagnetic devices that are not harmful, non-toxic, and non-invasive as well as non-toxic substances like herbs that are ingested. The FDA has assumed authority to approve the use of all medical protocols, and doctors can be harshly disciplined if they use therapies, or new remedies, not yet approved by the FDA. This, along with the controlling force of wealthy pharmaceutical companies who want to insure the public stays interested in their products, has put a stranglehold on the development of therapies that can't be patented. Similar to Brazil, where healers keep a low profile, and don't advertise their successes, practitioners of effective energy medicine in the US, sometimes feel it is best to remain quiet.

The FDA and AMA (American Medical Association) can rest assured that there are still many who categorically believe that anyone claiming to do healing through an electromagnetic device, or spiritual healing, must be a fraud—without examining the evidence. As spiritual healing becomes more integrated into our culture, it will be a challenge to create appropriate laws to protect qualified spiritual healers, promote viable research in Energy Medicine, and at the same time, protect consumers from those who are not qualified to practice healing.

Spiritists in Brazil have had to confront these issues. Perhaps their uphill struggle has added to their strength and clarity. Hopefully, we can learn from their history. Following is a brief recounting of a problem spiritual healers in Brazil have had vis a vis their laws, taken from Hess's "*Spirits and Scientists.*"

Until the late 1980s, Spiritist acitivities were considered illegal by the military dictatorship in political power. Even though politics has changed, and the current president was democratically elected by the people, neither the Brazilian government nor its medical authorities fully sanction the healing work of Kardecismo in Brazil.

In fact, a legal loophole remains that is threatening to anyone acting as a healer: the "curandeirismo" (translation: medicine man) law. The curandeirismo law is so broadly defined, agents of the law are in a position to prosecute any healer, with or without proof of his being a charlatan or fraud. Under the law agents can prosecute any healer or health practitioner who:

- habitually prescribes, administers, or applies any substance;
- uses gestures, words, or any other means;
- makes a medical diagnosis.

The penalty for breaking the curandeirismo law is detention for a period from six months to two years. A medium who practices surgery, like John of God, who physically operates on a patient while channeling a discarnate surgeon, clearly violates the curandeirismo law. But all Spiritist healers could be prosecuted for practicing spiritual healing, as well, under this same law.

Legal opinions on the strength of this law differ. Some lawyers understand the Spiritist energy pass as similar to a priest's blessing, and thus believe it can not be prosecuted, as it represents a "religious freedom." Practitioners of energy medicine also legitimize Spiritist healing by giving it the approval of science. Proponents of this point of view have even proposed a law that would require parapsychologists be represented on the faculties of medicine and psychology at schools and universities throughout Brazil.

During the 1980's, the federally mandated restrictions were even stricter. Public health regulations forbade the practice of religious therapy in Brazil's psychiatric hospitals. "Religious institutions of doctrinary sects and related associations are forbidden the practice, in psychiatric establishments, of their religion and any liturgical acts having therapeutic ends." Hess believed it is likely their intent was to ban the Spiritist treatment of "spirit obsession" in dozens of Spiritist owned psychiatric hospitals.

Even though this means that spiritual healing *can* be legally banned in Brazil, spiritual healing has been on the increase. John of God continues to work in his sanctuary; news media continue to cover his good works.

As science progresses, more evidence comes forward that spiritual healing and Energy Medicine have a scientific basis and are valuable components for both healing and health maintenance[2]. Spiritual healing in the form of Reiki, a Japanese form of laying-on of hands, is being endorsed in modern day hospitals in the United States. Touch for Health and Therapeutic Touch, all similar to Reiki, stemming from the study of spiritual healing in the East, are being taught in over a hundred conventional schools of nursing in the United States.[3]

I hope that in the future researchers will document the successes and positive potential of Kardecist Spiritism, and encourage the Brazilian government to reconsider the unreasonable limitations in their laws that threaten the good work done in their Spiritist Centers. There is much we can all learn from this very sophisticated philosophy and action-oriented path of personal evolution and healing. Perhaps the laws and certification programs that take root in other cultures will inspire Brazil to find a way to honor their own Spiritist Centers.

May we work together, sharing resources to make the most effective, economical therapies available to all people.

Summary

The Five Models of Spiritist Centers and Suggestions for Implementation

Following is a brief summary of the five different models of Spiritist Centers described in earier in the text.

Centro

Centro is located in downtown San Paulo. It is especially known for its sense of family, as it was started by a family who spent over twenty years together, studying Kardec, and volunteering at a center that was already functioning well. Similar to a functional family, there is openness to people of all religious faiths; there is open dialogue within the group; and there is a high quality of care devoted to everyone who "belongs to the family—" i.e. a member in classes and frequenter of activities at the center. Centro is also blessed by having a mentor who is considered to be one of the best mediums in Brazil. Along with her exceptional skills as a medium, she is ethical and highly disciplined, and, at the same time, tender and affectionate. She exercises her power by empowering other mediums in their training, and using her clairaudient and clairvoyant strengths in service to those seeking healing and/or messages from the departed. At Centro one learns to focus on his/her own personal transformation, transforming personal motivation from selfishness to service to others. Students of various levels develop increasing ability to personally connect with more highly evolved spirit guides.

As is typical of most centers, services of the center are born by small groups, rather than one or two charismatic leaders.

Busca Vida

Busca Vida is in the suburbs of a large city, Brasilia. It is a contemporary and unique adaptation of a Spiritist Center. Its mission is to give compassionate care to the ill and strengthen people who are on the path of personal transformation. The electromagnetic devices of Paul Laussac replace the use of energy passes by human hands. The only literal education offered is one or two hours of presentation on "How the Mind Works" to encourage each patient to take responsibility for orienting his/her thinking in a positive way. Other classes stimulate healthful living through specific exercise: Chi Kung, T'ai Chi, and Yoga. Kardec's books are not evident here, although portraits of Spiritist leaders are displayed on the walls.

Palmelo

Palmelo is a village of three thousand people in the country, over two hours drive from a major city. The center has a large assembly room for public functions, e.g. dis-obsession, readings in medical intuition, sessions for automatic writing. Activities of the center also take place in other buildings: a freestanding psychiatric institution, a classroom building, an orphanage for abandoned elders, and a daycare center. The Center's mediums perform psychic surgery and 'energy passes' on patients who stay in various independent Inns. Classes are offered in the philosophy of Spiritism as well as skill building for mediumship and healing.

One man, Damo, and his wife, Vania, are central figures managing the education of mediums and healers, performing medical intuition, directing public dis-obsession, giving private consultations and automatic writing to provide messages from the departed. Innkeepers who attend visitors and patients undergoing healing are mediums. They supervise the care of the Center's patients by managing meals, providing colonics as necessary, and leading group discussions and study groups at the Inns. Other mediums come in for scheduled visits with the patients. Patients are given clear indication of their diagnosis by Damo, prior to healing.

Abadiania

The Casa de Dom Inácio is located in a rural village of seventeen thousand people, two hours drive from Brasilia. This sanctuary is set up to support the work of one medium-healer, John of God. This extraordinary man sees up to one thousand people a day, who come to visit him from all over the world. John of God sometimes offers physical surgery while he is channeling a disincarnate, who was a surgeon in a prior life. Over thirty-three different entities come through John of God offering diagnosis and treatment protocols to visitors. Consultations are typically less than one minute in length. Physical surgeries last minutes, not hours. Visitors are not given a diagnosis, and sometimes don't even know why they are receiving a particular psychic surgery.

Treatments on site include: herbal remedies, crystal bed treatments (where electric light is pulsed through natural crystals onto the seven energy centers of the body), long meditation/prayer in meditation rooms, drinking blessed water, receiving psychic surgery, and bathing in a sacred waterfall for purification. Details of this Center, including interviews with patients and board-certified physicians who visited there, are in my (2002) book titled, "*Spiritual Alliances: Discovering the Roots of Health at the Casa de Dom Inácio.*"

FEESP

FEESP is in downtown San Paulo, a city of over seventeen million people. This Center is impressive by the quantity of activities and the number of people it serves. Seven thousand people come each day for either classes or energy passes. FEESP is able to also accomplish outreach through its own TV and radio stations, documentary films created on site, newspaper, lending library, and well-stocked bookstore. FEESP provides a central authority for the organization and overseeing of many satellite Spiritist Centers throughout Brazil. A large administrative body manages the organization of nine levels of classes for the public as well as a reception area/healing center that receives people twelve hours a day.

FEESP, like the other Spiritist Centers, has not documented case studies to prove the effectiveness of the medium/healers there, but it has documented that ninety-five percent of addicts and suicidally depressed who regularly come to FEESP regain emotional balance and a healthy lifestyle.

Following are parameters to help in beginning a Center:

Be Clear About the Physical Support You Need to Accomplish Your Mission: If you want to offer something to the community in the arena of healing and education, you need a place to meet. You need money for rent, or the purchase of a space, as well as appropriate furnishings to support the services you are providing. A computer, a telephone, and office supplies will be necessary. You need people who can maintain the physical place (janitorial service), and the organization of activities (administration). You need qualified teachers and a mentor to supervise the on-going development of these teachers. It's a good idea to start small, and grow as you have the financial and human resources available to support the organization.

About Finances: If you cultivate the ethical principles described in the "Gospel Explained by Spiritist Doctrine," and you put your faith in the guidance you receive from highly evolved spirits, Brazilian Spiritists believe you will be given sufficient money to proceed. This is a Law of Nature. If you want to start a Spiritist Center your faith is the most important element. You need to have faith that you will receive the help you need. This help comes from many dimensions.

About Charging a Fee for Services: No individual can be allowed to accept any fees for services as a healer or medium.

Be open to all people. The Center may accept donations only.

About Donations: Accept donations, but do not ask for them. Be circumspect about the donations you are offered. Do not accept "political" donations where there are strings attached, i.e. something that you must do in return for receiving the donation that is not an expression of the mission of your Center.

Be accountable with money. Be aligned with the laws of your governing bodies regarding creating and maintaining a non-profit organization.

Be Dedicated in Your Specific Mission: Spiritist Centers in general are dedicated to assist the poor and ill, as well as support the personal spiritual evolution of all people coming to the center. They accomplish these tasks as a group effort. Rarely does one charismatic leader step into the limelight to be supported by others who are not allowed to perform healings, use their mediumship skills, or teach. In this way all problems are born by a group, and all successes are group successes. This avoids the problem of one or more people using the center as a platform to promote their personal ego agenda.

Just as the dandelion starts from a small seed, allow your Center to start small. Just as the dandelion grows from seed to flower and leaf, allow your Center to take its unique shape. Just as the dandelion has its seasons of growth and transformation, allow your Center also to grow through its seasons—ultimately putting energy into creating more seeds that can form new Centers supporting spiritual evolution and healing in other environments.

Glossary

Apparitions: objects or beings that appear in non-physical form

Aura: energy field surrounding the body, visible in color to some mediums

Automatic writing: the act of both stopping volitional control of one's hands and allowing the intelligence of a disincarnate being to express itself through your ability to write.

Chakra: (Sanskrit for "wheel") links subtle energy bodies to the physical body. Considered to be a vortex of energy within the subtle body.

Clairsentience: a psychic gift which enables a medium to accurately feel what others are feeling in sensation and emotion without prior information or evidence.

Clairvoyance: a psychic gift that allows a medium to see subtle perceptions beyond the limitations of the normal physical sense of vision. This might include seeing energy fields, seeing visions of the future, seeing what someone has experienced in the past, or seeing with x-ray vision into the body.

Conscious: content of the mind that is in awareness.

Delta: a very low brain wave frequency, denoting a deeply relaxed state of mind. A person in Delta may be asleep. Highly evolved meditation practitioners reach Delta while awake, and are often in Delta when they are having paranormal experiences.

De-Possession: the act of causing the disincarnate to leave the body of the human being it is occupying. This may entail "educating the entity," i.e. teaching it where it is and what options it has for further growth and happiness.

Disincarnate: a being who is alive but not in a physical body; an entity without a body.

Dis-obsession: the act of stopping negative habitual patterns of thought inspired by disincarnates, so as to re-establish a person's free will and free-thinking.

Dowsing: the act of searching for information (usually locating water or minerals) with the use of a forked, green stick, a rod, or a pendulum. Implements like these, used for dowsing, are believed to move to indicate the direction of what is sought, or to indicate a "yes" or "no" answer. Movement seems to be generated by a subtle energy expressing the wisdom that is beyond the limitations of the conscious mind.

Ectoplasm: energy from spiritual dimensions or particular spirits that can take on a material form. This can happen in the presence of a medium invoking a spirit. The substance is called ectoplasm. It may appear emanating out of the mouth or ears of the medium. To the touch, ectoplasm has been reported as soft and elastic.

Ecumenism: A principle born out of the desire to foster connection, appreciation of diversity, and acceptance of brotherhood amongst all human beings. Spiritist Centers are ecumenical in that everyone can evolve to perfection by following Natural Laws, like cause and effect. They are independent of beliefs ascribed to by the followers of certain churches and synagogues. The dogmatic position, "without (a certain) church, there is no salvation" fosters separation, hatred and persecution.

Energy Healing: a practice whereby a health practitioner attends to the well being of the body through balancing energies.

Energy Passes: (Passé in Portuguese) Direct transmission of energy through a medium to a person. The energetic resources come from the dimension of spiritual entities, perhaps from specific entities.

Etheric Body: closely linked to the physical body, innermost part of the body's energy field (aura). Disturbances here correspond to problems in the physical body.

Fraternity of the Disciples of Jesus: a group of individuals honored by particular Spiritist leaders, i.e. Armond, as being particularly dedicated to assisting those who suffer from emotional and/or physical illness, including those needing help in their process of spiritual evolution.

Homeopathy: a method of treating disease by minute doses of organic substances that in a healthy person would produce symptoms similar to those of the disease. The originator, Hahnemann, believed that illness is due to a disturbance in the life force of the body and his remedies neutralized that disturbance.

Incorporation: (as in incorporation of spirits) the ability to allow a disincarnate being to use one's own physical body for a certain purpose, e.g. John of God incorporates a disincarnate surgeon who performs surgery on a patient using John's hands.

Laying-On of Hands: a form of healing claiming to work through channeling the healing energy of the universe through the healer for the benefit of the one being healed.

Magnetic passes: (magnetic healing). A transmission of energy mediated by one or more healers which balances the energy of the body with that of the energy field external to the body. Damo, a Spiritist leader in Palmelo, said, "I can't describe it in words. You can't tell where it starts and where it stops". We know that the energy Damo uses in magnetic passes can heal people sitting four to eight feet away from him. He refers to it as "shifting energy."

Magnetism: the science dealing with magnetic phenomena; this can include the science associated with addressing the energies of the body in healing. F.A. Mesmer made history in the late 19th century using 'animal magnetism' for healing purposes and hypnosis.

Meditation: a discipline using focusing techniques of the mind to relax body/mind and open awareness to diverse levels of consciousness. The goal is to move consciousness beyond ego. Varieties of this discipline have been used for over 4,000 years.

Mind: that which operates through intelligence (rational, sequential thinking) but is capable of awareness that is multi-dimensional and larger than the intellect, e.g. intuition, healing abilities, higher states of consciousness are contained in the mind. Mind has the capacity to direct the use of the body, intelligence and emotion through the will.

Muscle-testing: (aka Kinesiology) in the early 1970's when Dr. George Goodheart found that benign physical stimuli, e.g. a beneficial nutritional supplement, would increase the strength of certain indicator muscles, e.g.

the deltoid muscle, and inimical stimuli, e.g. chemical sweetener, would cause those same muscles to weaken. John Diamond, MD. had found that subjects universally test weak when listening to deceits, and strong when hearing demonstrably true statements.

Naturopath: health practitioner who maximizes life force to restore health and wellness. A number of treatments are used including diet, supplements, exercise, stress management, and hydrotherapy.

Obsession: one or more spiritually undeveloped disincarnates can cause a person to habitually think in certain ways. This person finds it increasingly difficult to listen and hear another person. He/she becomes increasingly more self-absorbed.

Paranormal: Phenomena that do not fit into the contemporary model of material cause and effect are referred to as paranormal. Researchers in psi phenomena see their job as finding the universal laws that govern these phenomena. The study of aspects of the paranormal having to do specifically with the mind are studied in parapsychology.

Parapsychology: the academic study of psychic faculties, particularly extra-sensory perception, mental telepathy and psycho-kinesis. It includes all paranormal phenomena in which the mind is involved, including clairvoyance, precognition, remote viewing, dowsing and healing. The word, "Parapsychology" was coined in the 1930's by Dr. J.B. Rhine, who did research at Duke University on the above phenomena.

Perfection: a spiritual state and an ability marked by such loving compassion that one can love all people, including doing good to those who hate us and praying for those who persecute us. "Everything that over-inflates our ego destroys or at least weakens the elements of true love, i.e., doing good, being tolerant, showing selfless dedication and devotion to others....the degree to which we are perfect is in direct relation to how far we can extend our love. It was for this reason that Jesus, having given His disciples the rules of the most sublime love said to them, 'Be perfect, as your heavenly Father is perfect.'" (*The Gospel Explained by Spiritist Doctrine*)

Peri-spirit: the semi-material aspect of spirit, or spiritual energy, that inhabits the body and leaves the body at death. It is sometimes conceived of as a sheath around the spirit, housing the immortal soul.'

Perennial Wisdom: comprehension of enduring, universal themes that every person must come to terms with in life, e.g. understanding the nature of death.

Personal transformation: ("reforma intima" in Portuguese) the task of becoming aware of and subsequently letting go of habits of thinking and behaving that are not motivated by compassion for oneself or others.

Personality: the qualities that make a person unique, or individual. One identifies strongly with one's personality at early stages of spiritual evolution. As one evolves to more expanded levels of consciousness, one becomes increasingly less identified with one's personality, more empathic, and more deeply connected to all of life.

Poltergeist: also known as Recurrent Spontaneous Psychokinesis. A certain spirit interacts with the material world in such way as to produce noises. Objects may be thrown around or appear from nowhere. Marks or writing may appear on walls. Machinery may break down.

Possession: a disincarnate of negative intent enters the body of a human being and takes control of his/her behavior, thinking and status of health.

Psi-phenomenon: events related to acquiring knowledge through the "sixth sense," without getting cues from the external five senses. Examples: mental telepathy, automatic writing, healing at a distance, channeling, psychokinesis, clairsentience, clairvoyance and clairaudience.

Psychokinesis: (abbreviated as "PK") was defined by Thalbourne as "the direct influence of mind on a physical system without the mediation of any known physical energy. This is considered in short form as "mind over matter" or the ability to move objects by thought or will-power alone.

Psychometry: the alleged ability to divine facts concerning a person or object by means of contact with or proximity to the object (Webster's Dictionary).

Psychotronic: devices that reflect on or impact the energy system of the body or the mind, e.g. cameras that photograph the energy field of the body, are psychotronic devices.

Reading: (as in, a medium "giving a reading") Certain mediums use clairsentience, clairaudience, and/or clairvoyance to report things about a person without having prior knowledge, e.g. medical problems, emotional issues, current feelings, past experiences. Some mediums use their clairaudient ability to listen to spirit guides who report information about the individual who is receiving the reading.

Reforma Intima: a Portuguese term correlating to the English "personal transformation"

Reiki: a hands-on, light-touch healing method developed in Japan at the beginning of the 20 century by Mikao Usui.

Reincarnation: The notion that the soul is immortal, moving alternately through a lifetime in the body to a lifetime in the spirit world, then again, another life in the body, and so on, until spiritual perfection in the human realm is reached. At this end point, a soul no longer needs to manifest on earth for further spiritual evolution.

Given that God is just and loves humanity, it would be unjust and illogical for individual life circumstances to be so varied if they were granted one lifetime only. One lifetime would never be sufficient to make the spiritual progress needed to find perfection. (See Appendix One.)

Rejuvenation device: in the context of this book, a rejuvenation device refers to an electric apparatus sending healing energy into the body to promote health.

Remote Viewing: psychically projecting awareness to observe objects or people at a distance. It has been used for spying during warfare, as well as medical diagnosis.

Re-orientation: Spiritists believe that many people who are unhappy, emotionally disturbed or physically ill need to study Spiritist principles and reevaluate their priorities in life. When one decides that brotherly love is the highest priority in life, and changes thinking and behavior to accommodate that priority, while continuing to study the Laws of Life, one is in the process of "re-orientation."

Séance: a French word, meaning 'sitting,' refers to a gathering of a circle of people including a medium for the purpose of communicating with spirits.

Shamanism: the oldest healing tradition, at least 50,000 years old, and an aspect of every indigenous culture. Shamans believe everything in the universe is alive and therefore has a spirit, which can detach from its physical form and move about freely. Shamans use very diverse modes of healing and convey wisdom from their knowledge of many levels of consciousness.

Soul: an incarnate spirit, that part of human intelligence that survives death and continues to live in a realm invisible to most humans.

Spiritism: originally the name for Spiritualism in Europe, and also the name still used by those in Brazil and the Phillipines who follow the codified principles of Spirits, collated by Allan Kardec, in the late 19th century.

Spiritualism: a religious movement that focuses on communications between human beings and disincarnate spirits. Spiritualism differentiated itself from Spiritism over the idea of reincarnation. Many Spiritualists thought reincarnation was inimical to Christian beliefs. All Spiritists believe in Reincarnation and consider that it is included in Christian belief.

Sub-conscious: that part of the mind that is below conscious control and/or below consciousness awareness. It automatically regulates the body, e.g. heart rate.

Subtle energy body/bodies: make up of the aura; invisible to most people, the energy body can be perceived and measured by sensitive modern instrumentation. It is a radiation of the physical body and the energetic imprint of the soul, which envelop the physical body in layers.

Super-conscious: that part of the mind that holds positive human potential, e.g. paranormal powers, including a feeling of Oneness with all of life.

Trans-cranial Electro-stimulator: an electrical stimulation device able to send an extremely low frequency current from one electrode placed on one side of the head, to another electrode on the other side. The goal of the electrical stimulation is therapeutic. Results vary but may include relief from addiction, anxiety, and depression. The therapy is painless. The results may last well after the device is used.

Transmigration: passing into another body at the time of death.

Will: in the context of Spiritist activity, "will" refers to that quality of Mind that chooses and sticks to a decision, e.g. she had to use her will to learn how to stay focused. "Goodwill" refers to a decision to be compassionate and caring.

Appendix One

How Christianity Relates to the Concept of Reincarnation

Reincarnation is fully accepted by the majority of people throughout the world.[1] The notion of reincarnation weaves like a golden thread through indigenous cultures, the oldest traditions of Western civilization, as well as throughout the Near and Far East—including Hinduism, Buddhism and esoteric Judaism.

They see life as a continuum, with birth and death the two doorways into and out of our earth phase. Birth, death and rebirth — the spiral turns around and around, seemingly in the same circle, but steadily rising upwards, until we refine the dross in our nature into the pure gold of spirit.

We so often think of life and death as opposites. Why has reincarnation remained on the fringes of acceptance amongst Christians in Europe and North America?

There is solid evidence that during its first centuries, Christianity did indeed teach that souls existed before this particular life (pre-embodiment) and would exist again in another life when this life is over (re-embodiment). In the first century AD, Josephus, the Jewish historian records in *Jewish War* and in his *Antiquities of the Jews* that reincarnation was taught widely in his day. Philo Judaeus, his contemporary, also refers to re-embodiment in one form or another.

There are also passages in the New Testament that can be understood only if seen against the background of the pre-existence of souls as a generally held belief. For instance, *Matthew* (16:13-14) records that when Jesus asked his disciples "Whom do men say that I am?" they replied that some people said he was Elijah, or Jeremiah, or another of the prophets. Later in *Matthew* (17:13), Jesus tells his disciples that John the Baptist was Elijah.

John (9:2-4) relates that the disciples asked Jesus whether a man born blind had to endure his blindness because he had sinned. Jesus replied that the works of God were made manifest in the blind man. Some interpret this as meaning that the law of cause and effect was being fulfilled, as St. Paul said, "we reap what we sow." Since the man was born blind he could not have sown the seeds of his blindness in his present body, but must have done so in a previous lifetime.

The earliest Christians, especially those who were members of one or another of the Gnostic sects, such as the Valentinians, Ophites or Ebionites, included re-embodiment among their important teachings. For them reincarnation enabled fulfillment of the law of karma, that every action has an effect, or a consequence. They believed reincarnation also provided the means for the soul to purify itself from the egoism developed in early stages of spiritual evolution.

The early Fathers of the Church, such as Justin Martyr (AD 100-l65), St. Clement of Alexandria (AD 150-220), and Origen (AD 185-254) also taught the pre-existence of souls and reincarnation. Examples are scattered through Origen's works, especially *Contra Celsum* (1, xxxii), where he asks: "Is it not rational that souls should be introduced into bodies, in accordance with their merits and previous deeds. . . ?" And in *De Principiis* he says that "the soul has neither beginning nor end."

St. Jerome (AD 340-420), translator of the Latin version of the Bible known as the *Vulgate,* in his *Letter to Demetrias* (a Roman matron), states that some Christian sects in his day taught a form of reincarnation as an esoteric doctrine, imparting it to a few "as a traditional truth which was not to be divulged."

Synesius (AD 370-480), Bishop of Ptolemais, also taught the concept. In one of his prayers, he writes: "Father, grant that my soul may merge into the light, and be no more thrust back into the illusion of earth." Others of his Hymns, such as number III, contain lines clearly stating his views, and also pleas that he may be so purified that rebirth on earth will no longer be necessary. In a thesis on dreams, Synesius writes: "It is possible by labor and time, and a transition into other lives, for the imaginative soul to emerge from this dark abode." This passage reminds us of verses in the *Revelation of John* (3:12), with its symbolic, initiatory language leading into: "Him that overcometh will I make a pillar in the temple of my God, and he shall go no more out."

Recall what happened after Emperor Constantine declared Christianity to be the state religion of the Roman Empire: The Church forgot the injunction about rendering unto Caesar the things that are Caesar's only, and allowed itself to become entwined with the administration of Caesar's realm. The destiny of the Church then became linked to the fate of the Empire and its rulers. In 325 AD Constantine formed a council of historians and scholars, the Council of Nicea, to modify Christian texts. Twenty-five texts were removed from the Bible, others were edited. The idea was to make the books have greater meaning to the common reader, so some of the deleted texts were reserved for the eyes of scholars only.

However, provincial political disturbances under weak emperors in the fourth century, and differences in teachings among the Christian sects continued. When the Byzantine Emperor, Justinian (483-565 AD), took charge of the Roman Empire in 527, he had to work desperately to reunify the crumbling Empire, and proceeded to do so on two fronts. First, he took military control of smaller states. Second, he attempted to enforce a uniform canon of religious belief, to be strictly adhered to.

The story of how all mention of reincarnation was deleted from the Bible is mired in the military and political controls and social intrigue of Justinian's rule. Essentially, Justinian reconstituted the foundational beliefs of the Church of Rome by authorizing severe editing of Biblical texts and Church records.

Here is the story: The Vatican, just recovering from having been subjugated by Theodoric the Ostrogoth, was under the "police protection" of Justinian's army, thus again subjugated by a military leader.

Theodora, a talented actress, known for being promiscuous, had gained favor with Justinian and become his wife. She followed the doctrine of the Monophysites, part of the Eastern Christian Church. This group rejected the teachings of the early Christian Church Fathers who followed Origen's beliefs in re-embodiment (reincarnation). As a result of this and other theological debates, the Monophysites of the Eastern Church had split from the Western Church Fathers.

In 451 AD a Church council issued the Chalcedonian Decree determining that Christ was both human and Divine, consistent with Origen's teachings. But, Theodora, now an Empress, had gained such power (contriving the murder of two Popes and finally installing her own selection, Pope Virgilius in 538 AD) that she influenced her husband to discredit and condemn all Origen's teachings, including the Chalcedonian Decree.

After Theodora's death in 547, Justinian, (whom historians consider to be mentally unstable and completely under the control of his tyrannical wife), was determined to deify both Theodora and himself. He committed himself to removing any aspect of Christian belief that would not allow that deification. Therefore, re-embodiment that reflected on the positive or the negative someone had achieved in previous lives had to be removed from Christian texts. Neither he nor his wife, were known for their beneficence, and could not have achieved the spiritual status of deification if they were to be judged on their prior good works.

Justinian convened the Fifth Ecumenical Church Council in 553AD. He invited 159 bishops of the Eastern Church (presumably all Monophysites) and only six bishops of the Western Church (all from Africa). When Pope Virgilus attempted to demand equal representation, it was refused. The Pope was not present at the deliberations, nor was he represented. The President of the Council was Eutychius, Patriarch of Constantinople, a puppet of Justinian. The Council was, in truth, a secular council attending to the sacred matters of the church.

No formal records of this Council were kept except proof of the legalization of a relatively unimportant and cursory matter, the "Three Chapters Edict" against three "heretics." At the same time, unreported by the Church scribes, a drama was taking place that determined new foundations of the Christian Church. During the meeting the Chalcedonian Decree of 451 was dissolved and all signs of Origen's teachings on reincarnation in the Christian Church were authorized to be erased. *The Bishops attending the council obediently subscribed to the "15 Anathemas" proposed by Justinian a reprint follows at the end of this narrative).* This kind of control was not hard to achieve when the Church was under the rule of the Emperor, and there were few books, almost all of which were in the monasteries and church libraries. They could be changed; pages could be burned.

Justinian made it appear that these changes had ecumenical endorsement or sanction. The opposition to Origen's teachings, mainly the one dealing with the pre-existence of souls, thus secured an official condemnation, and through military rule, they tried to make binding.

This rejection of pre-existence of the soul and, by implication, of reincarnation has never been reconsidered in over 1400 years. The issue of the restrictive editing of the teachings of the Christian Church under the authority of Justinian has never been re-examined by a properly authorized Ecumenical Council.

Virgilus and the next four Popes who followed after him do not refer to the condemnation of Origenism. Pope Gregory the Great (590-604 AD) made no reference to Origen. He accepted the trend toward codification of Christian belief that had been developing during the sixth century. Even in 1054, when the Roman and Greek churches excommunicated each other, Justinian's changing of the Biblical texts was not addressed.

The Old and New Testaments most commonly in use today date back to the version authorized by this very same Fifth Ecumenical Congress of Constantinople.

Thus, from the point of view of public teaching, the idea of reincarnation disappeared from European thought after this Fifth Council of 553AD. (Christian theologians say this happened on the grounds that it conflicted with a proper understanding of the concept of redemption.)

Despite the Fifth Council's endorsement of Justinian's new codification, evidence of Origen's ideas on reincarnation have continued to flow down the centuries like a steady stream through Christians leaders. From Maximus of Tyre (580-662) and Johannes Scotus Erigena (810-877), the erudite Irish monk… to St. Francis of Assisi, founder of the Franciscan Order (1182-1226), and St. Buonaventura, the 'Seraphic' doctor (1221-1274), who became a cardinal and General of the Franciscans. No less a theologian than St. Jerome said of Origen that he was "the greatest teacher of the early Church after the Apostles."

Apart from Christian sects like the widespread Cathars that included the Albigenses, Waldenses and Bomogils, isolated individuals — such as Jacob Boehme, the German Protestant mystic, Joseph Glanvil, chaplain of King Charles II of England, the Rev. William Law, William R. Alger, and many modern clerics, Catholic and Protestant — have supported the concept of reincarnation on logical and other grounds. Henry More (1614-1687), the noted clergyman of the Church of England and renowned Cambridge Platonist, wrote in his long essay *The Immortality of the Soul —*

a considerable study of the whole subject of the soul, with cogent answers to critics of pre-existency. His poem *A Platonick Song of the Soul* tells it beautifully:

> I would sing the Prae-existency
> Of humane souls, and live once o'er again
> By recollection and quick memory
> All that is past since first we all began.
> But all too shallow be my wits to scan
> So deep a point and mind too dull to clear
> So dark a matter, . . .

(Speaking then to Plotinus in the poem, he adds:)

> Tell what we mortalls are, tell what of old we were.
> A spark or ray of the Divinity
> Clouded in earthly fogs, yclad in clay,
> A precious drop sunk from Aeternitie,
> Spilt on the ground, or rather slunk away.

As More said in his essay mentioned above, "there was never any philosopher that held the soul spiritual and immortal but he held also that it did pre-exist."

Today's theologians are beginning to take a more open-minded stance upon the subject. When the Nag Hammadi Scrolls were discovered in 1945, and subsequently came under scrutiny by Biblical scholars[2], it became undeniable: the Bible as we came to know it is incomplete; reading what was formerly edited out leads us to new interpretations of the teachings of Jesus; we are still not certain who authored the books we call the Bible; and we must wonder if we have been misled. Religious scholars, like Elaine Pagels, who chaired the Department of Religion at Barnard College, have found substantial evidence that politics had a lot to do with how Biblical teachings have come to us.

Read the Gospel of Thomas, found in Nag Hammadi, and you see ancient Christian teaching that each human being has the potential to realize he/she is born out of the same seed as Christ, and can thus aspire to be self aware, understanding truth, and experiencing oneness with all things (what we ascribed to Levels of Initiation in Chapter Four). In this Gospel, Jesus says to Thomas:

> "Since it has been said that you are my twin and true companion, examine yourself so that you may understand who you are...I am the knowledge of the truth. So while you accompany me, although you do not understand (it), you already have come to know, and you will be called 'the one who knows himself.' For whoever has not known himself has known nothing, but whoever has known himself has simultaneously achieved knowledge about the depth of all things."

> Book of Thomas the Contender, 138.7-18
> In Nag Hammadi Library 189

Not only are clergy of varying denominations having to reconsider formerly unacceptable notions about our potential for spiritual evolution, and our personal intimate connection with Jesus; they must look more seriously at the ancient teachings about the pre-existence of the soul, re-embodiment in general, and reincarnation. The earlier rejection of reincarnation, based upon a misunderstanding of transmigration, has given way to a more intelligent inquiry. Scientists, like Gary Schwartz, PhD.[3][4] (formerly director of the Yale Psychophysiology Center and currently a professor of psychology, medicine and psychiatry, at the University of Arizona), Ian Stevenson, MD [5], (Carlson Professor of Psychiatry and Director of the Division of Personality Studies at the Health Sciences Center, University of Virginia), and Dean Radin, PhD.[6], Laboratory Director from the Institute of Noetic Sciences, are finding substantial evidence of life after death, and reincarnation. Thus, it is only reasonable that Christian clergy and Christians consider the possibility that our life alternates between life in a body and life as a spirit, constantly evolving.

Following are the 15 Anathemas, copied from *A Select Library of Nicene and Post-Nicene Fathers of the Christian Church,* Vol. 14, Series 2, entitled *"The Seven Ecumenical Councils of the Undivided Church,"* edited by Henry R. Percival, MA, DD (New York: Charles Scribner's Sons, 1900) pp 318-20. The words in brackets are Percival's own editing.

The Fifteen Anathemas Against Origen

If anyone assert the fabulous pre-existence of souls, and shall assert the monstrous restoration which follows from it: let him be anathema (cursed).

If anyone shall say that the creation of all reasonable things includes only intelligences without bodies and altogether immaterial, having neither number or name, so that there is unity between them all by identity of substance, force and energy, and by their union with and knowledge of God, the word; but that no longer desiring the sight of God, they gave themselves over to worse things, each one following his own inclinations, and that they have taken bodies more or less subtle, and have received names, for among the heavenly Powers there is a difference of names as there is also a difference of bodies; and thence some became and are called Cherubims, other Seraphims, and Principalities, and Powers, and Dominations, and Thrones, and Angels, and as many other heavenly orders as there may be: let him be anathema.

If anyone shall say that the sun, the moon, and the stars are also reasonable things, and that they have only become what they are because they turned towards evil: let him be anathema.

If anyone shall say that the reasonable creatures in whom the divine love had grown cold have been hidden in gross bodies such as ours, and have been called men, while those who have attained the lowest degree of wickedness have shared cold and obscure bodies and are become and called demons and evil spirits: let him be anathema.

If anyone shall say that a psychic condition has come from an angelic or archangelic state, and moreover that a demoniac and a human condition has come from a psychic condition, and that from a human state they may become again angels and demons, and that each order of heavenly virtues is either all from those below or from those above and below: let him be anathema.

If anyone shall say that there is a twofold race of demons, of which the one includes the souls of men and the other the superior spirits who fell to this, and that of all the number of reasonable beings there is but one which has remained unshaken in the love and contemplation of God, and that that spirit is become Christ and the king of all reasonable beings, and that he has created all the bodies which exist in heaven, on earth, and between heaven and earth; and that the world which has in itself elements more ancient than itself, and which exist by themselves, viz: dryness, damp, heat and cold, and the image to which it was formed, was so formed, and that the most holy and consubstantial Trinity did not create the world, but that it was created by the working intelligence which is more ancient than the world, and which communicates to it its being: let him be anathema.

If anyone shall say that Christ, of whom it is said that he appeared in the form of God, and that he was united before all time with God the Word, and humbled himself in those last days even to humanity, had (according to their expression) pity upon the diverse falls which had appeared in the spirits united in the same unity (of which he himself is part) and that to restore them he passed through divers classes, had different bodies and different names, became all to all, an Angel among Angels, a Power among Powers, had clothed himself in the different classes of reasonable beings with a form corresponding to that class, and finally has taken flesh and blood like ours and is become man for man; [if anyone says all this] and does not profess that God the World humbled himself and became man: let him be anathema.

If anyone shall not acknowledge that God the Word, of the same substance with the Father and the Holy Ghost, and who was made flesh and became man, one of the Trinity, is Christ in every sense of the word, but [shall affirm] that he is so only in an inaccurate manner, and because of the abasement, as they call it, of the intelligence; if anyone shall affirm that this intelligence united to God the Word, is the Christ in the true sense of the word, while the Logos is only called Christ because of this union with the intelligence, and e converso that the intelligence is only called God because of the Logos; let him be anathema.

If anyone shall say that it was not the Divine Logos made man by taking an animated body with a rational spirit (anima rationalis) and VOEPA, that he descended into hell and ascended into heaven, but shall pretend that it is the NOUS which has done this, that NOUS of which they say (in an impious fashion) he is Christ, properly called, and that he is become so by knowledge of the Monad: let him be anathema.

If anyone shall say that after the resurrection the body of the Lord was ethereal, having the form of a sphere, and that such shall be the bodies of all after the resurrection; and that after the Lord himself shall have rejected his true body and after the others who rise shall have rejected theirs, the nature of their bodies shall be annihilated: let him be anathema.

If anyone shall say that the future judgment signifies the destruction of the body and that the end of the story will be an immaterial [false appearance?] and that thereafter there will no longer be any matter, but only spirit: let him be anathema.

If anyone shall say that the heavenly Powers and all men and the Devil and evil spirits are united with the Word of God in all respects, as the NOUS which is by them called Christ and which is in the form of God, and which humbles itself as they say; and [if anyone shall say] that the kingdom of Christ shall have an end: let him be anathema.

If anyone shall say that Christ [i.e., the NOUS] is in no wise different from other reasonable beings, neither substantially nor by wisdom nor by his power and might over all things but that all will be placed at the right hand of God, as well as he that is called by them Christ [the NOUS], as also they were in the feigned pre-existence of all things; let him be anathema.

If anyone shall say that all reasonable beings will one day be united in one, when the hypostases as well as the numbers and the bodies shall have disappeared, and that the knowledge of the world to come will carry with it the ruin of worlds, and the rejection of bodies as also the abolition of [all] names, and that there shall be finally an identity...of the hypostasis; moreover, that in this pretended apocatastasis, spirits only will continue to exist, as it was in the feigned pre-existence; let him be anathema.

If anyone shall say that the life of the spirits shall be like to the life which was in the beginning while as yet the spirits had not come down or fallen, so that the end and the beginning shall be alike, and that the end shall be the true measure of the beginning; let him be anathema.

If anyone does not anathematize Arius, Eunomius, Macedonius, Apollinaris, Nestorius, Eutyches and Origen, as well as their impious writings, as also all other heretics already condemned and anathematized by the Holy Catholic and Apostolic Church, and by the aforesaid four Holy Synods and (if anyone does not equally anathematize) all those who have held and hold or who in their impiety persist in holding to the end the same opinion as those heretics just mentioned: let him be anathema.

In writing the above Appendix I gathered much information from an article which first appeared in *Sunrise Magazine*, May, 1973, published by the Theosophical University Press. They used the following references:

The Ring of Return, An Anthology, by Eva Martin;
The Cathars and Reincarnation, by Arthur Guirdham;
Reincarnation, A Study of Forgotten Truth, by E. D. Walker;
Fragments of a Faith Forgotten, by G. R. S. Mead;
Reincarnation in World Thought, compiled by J. Head and S. L. Cranston;
The Esoteric Tradition, by G. de Purucker;
Essays and Hymns of Synesius, translated by Augustine Fitzgerald.
The Lost Books of the Bible and the Forgotten Books of Eden. New York: New American Library, 1963. (Several copies of this book are now available from other publishing houses.)

Footnotes

[1] Head, Joseph and Cranston, S.L. (editors). *Reincarnation in World Thought*, New York: Julian Press, 1967
[2] Elaine Pagels, *The Gnostic Gospels,* 1979.
[3] G. Schwartz, *The Afterlife Experiments,* 2002.
[4] G. Schwartz and D. Chopra, "*Science and Soul: The Survival of Consciousness After Death,*" an audiotape made in 2001.
[5] I. Stevenson, *Where Reincarnation and Biology Intersect,* 1997.
[6] D. Radin, *The Conscious Universe: The Scientific Truth of Psychic Phenomena,* 1997.

References

Afonsa, F. April 2002. "A Busca da Cura Espiritual," in *Planeta*, p. 12 -17.

Aria, Eduardo, March,2002, "A Incansavel Elsie," in *Planeta*, p. 36-41.

——————July, 2003, "O Genio a Ser Compreendido," in *Planeta*, p. 31-35.

Bohm, D.,1980. *Wholeness and the Implicate Order.* London: Routledge, Kegan & Paul.

Bragdon, E., 2002. *Spiritual Alliances: Discovering the Roots of Health at the Casa de Dom Inácio.* Woodstock, VT: Lightening Up Press.

Canadas, Cleide Martins, 2001. *A Eterna Busca da Cura.* San Paulo, Brasil: Boa Nova Editora.

Coelho, Paulo, 1994. *The Alchemist.* New York: HarperCollins. This well-loved Brazilian author has been translated into 55 different languages, and created #1 bestselling books in 39 countries. Coelho lives in San Paulo, Brazil, where he helps underprivileged children and the elderly through the Paulo Coelho Institute.

Don, Norman S, Moura, Gilda, 2000. "Trance Surgery in Brazil," in *Alternative Therapies, Vol.6, No.4, 39-48.*

Doyle, A. Conan, 1926. (2003 edition) *History of Spiritualism.* NL: Fredonia Books.

Eisenberg, DM, Davis, RB, Ettner, SL, Appel, S, Wilkey, S. Van Rampey, M & Kessler, RC,, 1998. "Trends in Alternative Medicine Use in the United States, 1990-1997" in *Journal of the American Medical Association*, Vol. 280. 1569-1575.

Eisenberg, DM & Kaptchuk, TJ, 2001. "Varieties of Healing 2: A Taxonomy of Unconventional Healing Practices" 2000, in *Annals of Internal Medicine.* Vol 135 (3), 196-204.

Fuller, J.G., 1974. *Arigo: Surgeon of the Rusty Knife.* New York: Thomas Crowell Company.

Gordon, J. 1996. *Manifesto for a New Medicine.* Reading, MA: Perseus Books.

Greenfield, S.M., 1994. A model explaining Brazilian Spiritist surgeries and other unusual, religious-based healings. *Subtle Energies. 5 (2):109-141.*

——————*1997.* The patients of Dr Fritz: assessments of treatments by a Brazilian Spiritist healer. *J. Soc Psychical Res.* 61: 372-383.

Haley, Daniel, 2000. *Politics in Healing: The Suppression and Manipulation of American Medicine*. Washington, DC: Potomac Valley Press.

Hawkins, David. 1995. *Power Versus Force: An Anatomy of Consciousness*. Sedona, AZ: Veritas Publishing

Head, J. and Cranston, S.L., 1961. *Reincarnation: an East-West Anthology*. Wheaton, Ill.: The Theosophical Publishing House.

Hess, David. 1991. *Spirits and Scientists*. Philadelphia: Pennsylvania State University Press.

—————-1983. *Samba in the Night: Spiritism in Brazil*. New York: Columbia University Press.

Jurriaanse, Aart 1974. *Of Life and Other Worlds*. Johannesburg, South Africa: World Unity and Service Trust

—————-1977, *Prophecies*. Johannesburg, SA: World Unity & Service Trust

—————-1978. *Bridges*. Pretoria, South Africa: Bridges Trust

Kalb, C, Underwood, A., Pierce, E, Raymond, J., Hontz, J, Springen, K and Childress, S. *"Faith and Healing"* a special section of *"God &Health"* in Newsweek, November 10, 2003.

Kardec, Allan. 1865 (English translation, 2000) *The Gospel Explained by the Spiritist Doctrine*. Philadelphia: Allan Kardec Educational Society

—————-1857 (English translation,1996). *The Spirits' Book*. Brasilia, Brasil: Federacao Espirita Brasileira

—————-1861. (English Translation, 1986). *The Mediums' Book*. Brasilia, Brasil: Federacao Espirita Brasileira.

Khalsa, DS & Stauth, C., 2001. *Meditation as Medicine*. NY: Simon & Schuster.

Langley, Noel 1967. *Edgar Cayce on Reincarnation*. New York: Warner Books.

Frank Lawlis, PhD, 2001, *Mosby's Alternative and Complementary Medicine: A Research Based Approach*

Martin, Harvey, 1999. *The Secret Teachings of the Espiritistas*. Savannah, GA: Metamind Publications.

Morata, Agnelo, 1991. *De Sacramento A Palmelo: Sacramento, Recanto do Luz- Ambiente de Euripedes Barsanulfo*. Sao Bernardo do Campo, Brazil: Edicoes Correio Fraterno.

National Foundation for Alternative Medicine (NFAM), Oct. 2003 *"Emerging Opportunities for Affordable Healthcare Solutions."* Washington, DC:NFAM.

Oschman, J., 2004. "Recent Developments in Bioelectromagnetic Medicine" in *Bioelectromagnetic Medicine,* Marcel Dekker, Inc.

——————————2003. *Energy Medicine in Therapeutics and Human Performance.* Philadelphia: Elsevier Science

——————————2000. *Energy Medicine: The Scientific Basis.* Philadelphia: Elsevier Science.

Pagels, Elaine. 1979. *The Gnostic Gospels.* NY: Random House.

Playfair, Guy Lyon. 1975. *The Flying Cow.* London: Souvenir Press.

——————————1976. *The Indefinite Boundary.* London: Souvenir Press.

Santos, Jose Luiz dos. 1997. *Espiritismo, uma religiao Brasilieiro.* San Paulo: Moderna.

Schwartz, G. with Simon, W. 2002. *The Afterlife Experiments: Breakthrough Scientific Evidence of Life After Death.* NY: Simon & Schuster.

Sheldrake, Rupert. 1981. *A New Science of Life.* Los Angeles, CA: Tarcher.

Watson, Donald. 1991. *A Dictionary of Mind and Spirit.* London: Andre Deutsch.

Xavier, Francisco. 1943. (English translation, 2000), *Nosso Lar-A Spiritual Home,* Philadelphia, PA: Allan Kardec Educational Society.

——————————1968. (English translation, 2000) *And Life Goes On.* Philadelphia, PA: Allan Kardec Educational Society.

Recommended Reading

Reading Specific to Exploring Reincarnation And Past Life Therapy

Gauld, Alan. 1984. *Mediumship and Survival: A Century of Investigations.* Chicago: Academy.

Grant, Joan & Kelsey, Denys, 1969. *Many Lifetimes: Concerning Reincarnation and the Origins of Mental Illness.* London: Victor Gollancz, Ltd.

Head, Joseph and Cranston, S.L. (editors) 1967. *Reincarnation in World Thought,* New York: Julian Press.

——————————1977. *Reincarnation: The Phoenix Fire Mystery.* New York: Crown Publishers

Langley, N., (H.L. Cayce as editor), 1967. *Edgar Cayce On Reincarnation.* New York: Warner Books.

Lucas, Winafred Blake (ed.), 1993. *Regression Therapy, A Handbook for Professionals, Vol I & II.* California: Deep Forest Press

Moody, R. with Perry, P. 1991. *Coming Back: A Psychiatrist Explores Past-Life Journeys.* New York: Bantam.

—————2001. *Life After Life.* NY: Harper SanFrancisco.

Motoyama, Hiroshi, 1992. *Karma and Reincarnation: The Key to Spiritual Evolution and Enlightenment.* London: Judy Piatkus, Ltd.

Newton, Michael, 1996. *Journey of Souls- Case Studies of Life Between Lives.* St. Paul, MN: Llewellyn Books.

Nowotny, Karl, 1972 (English translation, 1990). *Messages from a Doctor in the Fourth Dimension, Vol I & II.* London, England: Regency Press, Ltd. Dr. Karl Nowotny was born in 1895 in Vienna. He was a neurologist, psychiatrist and Assistant Professor at the University of Vienna. He died in 1965. Two years later, a friend of his who is a medium began channeling Nowotny's report of life after death. The intelligent, clear report of Nowotny paints an extraordinarily revealing picture of the fourth dimension. He was obviously already a highly evolved man prior to his death in 1965.

Radin, Dean. 1997. The Conscious Universe: The Scientific Truth of Psychic Phenomena. NY: HarperCollins.

Schwartz, G. with Simon, W. 2002. *The Afterlife Experiments: Breakthrough Scientific Evidence of Life After Death.* NY: Simon & Schuster.

Scott-Rogo, D. 1985. *The Search for Yesterday: A Critical Examination of the Evidence of Reincarnation.* New Jersey: Prentice Hall.

Spiegel, David, 1996. "Cancer and Depression" in British Journal of Psychiatry, 168 (supple. 30), 109-116.

Stemman, R., 1997. *Reincarnation: Amazing True Cases from Around the World.* London: Judy Piatkus, Ltd.

Stevenson, Ian. 1997. *Where Reincarnation and Biology Intersect.* Westport, CT: Praeger Publishers.
This is a summary of over 2,000 cases which give ample evidence for reincarnation.

—————1974, *Twenty Cases Suggestive of Reincarnation,* Charlottesville, VA: University Press of Virginia.

Weiss, B. 1992. *Through Time into Healing.* New York: Simon &Schuster.

—————1994. *Many Lives, Many Masters.* London: Piatkus Books

—————1996. *Only Love is Real.* NY: Warner Books

Whitton, Joel, and Fisher, Joe, 1986. *Life Between Life.* London: Grafton B ooks.

Woolger, Roger, 1988. *Other Lives, Other Selves.* New York: Bantam Books.

Reading Specific to Exploring Healing And Laying-On Of Hands

Barnett L. & Chamber, M., 1996. *Reiki: Energy Medicine.* Rochester, VT: Healing Arts Press.

Benor, D.J. 2001. *Spiritual Healing: Scientific Validation of a Healing Revolution.* Vision Publications.

Brennan, Barbara Ann, 1987. *Hands of Light: A Guide to Healing Through the Human Energy Field.* New York: Bantam.

—————1993. *Light Emerging: The Journal of Personal Healing.* New York: Bantam.

Dossey, Larry, 1993. *Healing Words.* San Francisco: HarperCollins.

Dziemidko, H., 1999. *The Complete Book of Energy Medicines.* Rochester, VT: Healing Arts Press.

Guirdam, Arthur, 1978, *The Psyche in Medicine.* England: C.W. Daniel, Ltd.

—————*Possession, Past Lives, Powers of Evil in Disease.* Jersey, Channel Islands: Neville Spearman (Jersey) Limited.

—————1980, *Paradise Found: Reflections on Psychic Survival.* Willingborough, Northamptonshire, England: Turnstone Press Ltd.

Karagulla, Shafica. 1967. *Breakthrough to Creativity: Your Higher Sense Perception.* Marina Del Rey, CA: DeVorss & Co.

—————1989. *The Chakras and the Human Energy Fields.* Wheaton, Ill.: The Theosophical Publishing House.

Karagulla, S. with Neal, V.P., 1993. (new edition) *Through the Curtain.* CA: DeVorss & Co.

Krippner, S. & Villoldo, A, 1987. *Healing States: A Journey into the World of Spiritual Healing and Shamanism.* New York: Simon & Schuster.

Krippner, S., Cardena, E. Lynne, S. (Editors), 2000. *Varieties of Anomalous Experiences.* Washington, DC: American Psychological Association.

Kunz, Dora 1991. *The Personal Aura.* Wheaton, Ill.: Theosophical Publishing House.

—————1985. *Spiritual Aspects of the Healing Arts.* Wheaton, Ill.: The Theosophical Publishing House.

Motoyama, H., 1989. *Theories of the Chakras.* Wheaton, Ill.: The Theosophical Publishing House.

Oschman, J., 2004. "Recent Developments in Bioelectromagnetic Medicine" in *Bioelectromagnetic Medicine,* Marcel Dekker, Inc.

——————2003. *Energy Medicine in Therapeutics and Human Performance.* Philadelphia: Elsevier Science

——————2000. *Energy Medicine: The Scientific Basis.* Philadelphia: Elsevier Science.

Footnotes

Introduction

[1] *Spiritists and Scientists*; and *Samba in the Night: Spiritism in Brazil*
[2] Leila Speeden in conversation, October, 2003.
[3] Afonsa, F. *"A Busca Da Cura Espiritual,"* in Planeta, April, 2002, p. 12-17.
[4] Bragdon, E. *"Spiritual Alliances: Discovering the Roots of Health at the Casa de Dom Inácio,"* 2001.
[5] Dan Haley, *"Politics in Healing,"* 2000, page 2.
[6] USA Today, April 24, 1998.
[7] Townsend Letter, May 1998.
[8] "Emerging Opportunities for Affordable Healthcare Solutions," October, 2003. Author: The National Foundation for Alternative Medicine
[9] Hawkins, D. *"Power versus Force,"* 1995.
[10] Haley, D., *"Politics in Healing,"* 2000, page 4.
[11] Ibid, page 7.
[12] Ibid, page 10.
[13] Eisenberg et al., "Trends in alternative medicine use in the US, 1990-1997," JAMA, 1998.
[14] NFAM Report, Ibid.
[15] Newsweek, Nov. 10, 2003. *"God and Health"*
[16] Ibid, p.48
[17] Ibid, p. 49
[18] Ibid, p.46
[19] personal conversation, February, 2004.

Chapter One

[1] Oschman, J. *"Energy Medicine in Therapeutics and Human Performance,"* 2003.
[2] Oschman, J. *"Energy Medicine: The Scientific Basis,"* 2000.
[3] Ibid., p. xiv.

Chapter Two

[1] Harvey Martin, *The Secret Teachings of the Espiritistas*, 1999.
[2] Translated for the author by Professor John Zerio, translator for the Allan Kardec Educational Society.
[3] David Hess, *Spiritists and Scientists*
[4] Martin, H. *The Secret Teachings of the Espiritistas*, p. 72.
[5] Ibid, p. 75.
[6] Watson, D. *A Dictionary of Mind and Spirit*, 1991.
[7] Stevenson, I., *"Where Reincarnation and Biology Intersect,"* 1997.
[8] Allan Kardec Educational Society (AKES), PO Box 26336, Philadelphia, PA 19141. Phone: 215-329-4010. www.allan-kardec.org

Chapter Three

[1] Miguel Bertolucci in his Preface to the *Gospel—Explained by Spiritist Doctrine*, p ix

Chapter Four

[1] David Hawkins, *Power versus Force,* 1995.
[2] D. Hawkins, *The Eye of the I,* 2001.
[3] Jurriaanse, A. *Bridges,* 1978.

Chapter Six

[1] See *Mosby's Complementary and Alternative Medicine: A Research Based Approach.*

Chapter Seven

[2] J Oschman, *Energy Medicine: The Scientific Basis.*

Chapter Ten

[1] G. Schwatrz, *The Afterlife Experiments: Breakthrough Scientific Evidence of Life After Death.*

Chapter Eleven

[1] Dan Haley, *Politics in Healing: The suppression and manipulation of American Medicine,* 2000.
[2] J. Oschman, *"Energy Medicine: The Scientific Basis,"* 2000.
[3] NFAM, October 2003.

Index

A

Abadiania *see* Casa de Dom Inácio
Acerola juice 62
activities, typical in Spiritist Centers 7–10
addiction *see* recovery from addiction
Afterlife Experiments: Breakthrough Scientific Evidence of Life After Death, The 111
AIDS x, 4, 85
    and Cellular Rejuvenator 74
    healing viii
Aksakof, Alexandre 112
Albuquerque, Marco de 67–68
Alcoholics Anonymous (Al-Anon) 98
alcoholism *see* recovery from addiction
Aliança 10
alternative health care
    for cancer treatment xi
    practitioners xi
    North Americans pursuing xiii
alternative health care centers, Spiritist Centers as 3
Alvear 21
American Medical Association (AMA) ix, 126, 127
anatomy of consciousness 38
Andrade, Hernani Guimaraes 24
Angels, ability to speak to viii, 21
animals, mediumship with 111
animism 112
Animism and Spiritism 112
anonymity in Spiritist Centers xiv, 6, 17, 81
antibiotic 9
anxiety, treatment of 72
Apostles 21
Armond, Edgard 24, 111, 115, 122, 124
art expositions, in Spiritist Centers 10
astral body vii
attention 42
attitude, positive 48, 63, 69, 72, 77
auras *see* subtle energy fields
automatic writing 8–9, 62, 79, 83, 108, 112

B

Bailar, J.C. ix
Bailey, Alice 39, 67, 93
Barbara Brennan School of Healing 13
Barsanulfo, Euripedes 56

Basic Course, the 83, 104–107, 118
    goal of 105–107
    labwork 108
Bedell, Berkley x, xi
bio-chemical
    model of health 11, 18
    protocols 12
bio-chemistry *see* biochemical model of health
bio-electromagnetic medicine 12
    see also Energy Medicine
biophysics, research in 10
black magic 22
Blavatsky, H. 67
blessed water, as an antibiotic 9
bookstores, in Spiritist Centers 10, 89, 107
Bosco, Dom 68
Brasilia, Brazil 10, 67
Brazil
    penal code banning Spiritism in 22
    popularity of Spiritism in 17
    shamanic tradition in 18
Brazilian Research Institute of Psycho-Biophysics 24
Bridges 38, 39
Bringing Together the Fraternities of the Universe with the Fraternities of Space 123
brotherhood 26–27, 34, 76, 85, 93
Busca Vida (Center of the Research of Life) 34, 50, 67–77, 132

C

cancer
    and Cellular Rejuvenator 73
    Centro, treatment at 86–87
    and electromagnetic devices 72–76
    healing viii, 4, 11, 69–72
    kidney 86
    metastasized, treatment of 69–70
    origins of 70–71, 86
    ovarian viii
    Panel Meeting ix
    psychosomatic component of 86
    research *see* research
    and stress 86
    war on ix, xii, 10, 75
Cancer Panel Meeting ix

cancer patients
  complementary and alternative health
    care xi
Candinho, Jeronimo 56
Candomble 22
Casa de Dom Inácio vii, viii, xiv, 25, 133
Casa, the see Casa de Dom Inácio
Cassileth, Barrie xi
Catholicism vii, 17, 60, 68
  coexistence with Spiritism 84
Catholic Church 18, 83
Cayce, Edgar 23
cell memory 73
cellular biology, research in 10
Cellular Rejuvenator 73–74
Center for Consolation and Inspiration
    see Centro
Center of the Research of Life see Busca Vida
Centers see Kardecist Spiritist Centers
Centro 79–88, 131
  anonymity at 81
  energy passes at 81
  fees for services at 80
  financial resources of 98–101
  money, raising at 98–100
  organizational structure of 97–98
  services available at 79
  volunteers at 80
Centro Consolação e Inspiração see Centro
chakras 110, 112
Chalcedonian Decree 148
channel 45
charity vii, 9, 19, 26, 106
  and children 107
  Fraternity of the Disciples of Jesus 24
  and financial support of Spiritist
    Centers 99
  and Spiritism 34
  and Spiritualism 30–31
  and teachers 117
  see also volunteering
Chi Kung 67, 68
children, and Spiritism 107
Chopra, Deepak 10
Christ 21
  significance of teachings of 20
  and Levels of Initiation 46
  mediumship of 111
Christianity
  principles in Kardec's books 64
  reincarnation and 145–155
  Spiritism, relationship to 19, 21, 34, 107
  Spiritualism, consistency with 21

chronic illnesses x
churches 13, 18
churchgoing xii
clairaudience 58, 112
clairvoyance 58, 112
clinical trials 101
  of complementary health protocols xii
  of energy passes 101
  of results in Spiritist Centers xiv
  of trans-cranial electro-stimulator 72
community health centers, and Spiritist
    Centers 96
community involvement xii, xiii, 19, 76
community centers, Spiritist Centers as 3
compassion 46, 77, 85
complementary health care xi, xii
  for cancer treatment xi
  clinical trials for xii
compulsions, healing of 8
  see also dis-obsession and de-possession
consciousness
  development of human 40
  anatomy of 38
  see also levels of consciousness
consultations, personal 8
cost of treatment see fees for services
Course for Mediumship, see Curso de Mediuns
courses, in Spiritist Centers 9
curandeirismo law 127–128
cure see healing
Curso de Mediuns (Course for Mediumship)
    110–115

D

Damo, Bartolo 55–65
Damo, Vania 62
Darque, Joaninha 55
de-possession 8, 59, 60
  and electromagnetic devices 69
death xiv, 87–88, 106
  caused by adverse reactions to drugs ix
  fear of xiv
  life after 105
  questions about 83
  rates for heart patients xii
  reduction in churchgoers xii
  soul's survival after 19, 21
Delanne, Gabriel 112
delta brain wave frequency 72
demographics of Spiritism 17
Denis, Leon 112
depression, treatment of 72

devices
certification of, for Energy Medicine 12
Superconducting Quantum
Interference 11
see also electromagnetic devices
devotion, at Emotional level 41
diagnosis
with measuring devices 11
by medical intuitives 8
non-invasive medical 5
see also medical intuition
Diamond, John 38
Director of Social Assistance, at Centro 97
divisions reporting to 98
Director of Philosophical Classes, at Centro
97, 117
leaders reporting to 98
dis-obsession 8, 59, 60, 91, 113
and electromagnetic devices 69
disease
as an alarm clock 65
psychosomatic component of 86
disincarnate beings *see* disincarnates
disincarnates 4, 5, 18, 22
communicating with 30, 49
and Levels of Initiation 46
negative 59, 60–61, 92
and origin of FEESP 122
treatment with energy passes 61
Divine *see* God
Divine Justice 106
DK 33, 39, 45, 50, 93, 115
doctrine of, Allan Kardec vii, 27
donations to Spiritist Centers 6, 95, 98–99,
100 134
dreams 5, 112
drug addiction *see* recovery from addiction
drug companies, USA xi
drugs, prescription
adverse reactions to ix
in combination with Spiritism 63
cost of ix, 99
research of xi
as medical intervention 11
Dubugras, Elsie, 7, 13, 22, 25
and Centro 86
and FEESP 92–93
and mediumship 114
religion, definition of 33
dying, care for the 13

Eadie, B.J. 46
East Indian philosophy vii
ecumenical *see* ecumenism
ecumenical schools, Spiritist Centers as 3
ecumenism xiii, 7, 28, 84, 148
Editora Tres 33
ego 48
avoiding inflation of 6
and mediumship 109, 111
egotism 36
electromagnetic devices xiii, 12, 67, 72, 69
consistency of 74
history of use 75
Laussac's 72–76
Russia 72
restrictions on by FDA 127
treatment with 72
electromagnetic energy 11
Embraced by the Light 46
emergency emotions 40
emergency medicine 11
Emmanuel 23
emotional disorders
healing for 8
treatment of vii, 11, 72
Emotional level 38, 41–42
emotional states, of Physical level of
consciousness 40
endorphins, and Levels of Initiation 48
*Energetic Passes and Radiations: Spiritual
Methods of Curing* 24, 111, 115
energy centers *see* chakras
energy fields 11
energy fields of consciousness 38
energy, forms of 10
Energy Medicine 10–13, 69
certification of devices for 12
model 11
restrictions on 126–127
scientific basis of 128
Energy Medicine: The Scientific Basis 10
energy passes 8, 58, 112
at Centro 81
electromagnetic devices, replacing 74–76
at FEESP 90
hyperactivity, treatment of 86
negative disincarnates,
treatment of 61, 62
Reiki, compared with 91
schizophrenia, treatment of 60

energy passes cont.
    training for 115–116
    see also laying-on of hands
entities *see* spirits
etheric body 61
    see also subtle energy fields
Euripedes Barsanulfo Hospital 56, 60, 64
evocation 50
evolution
    of human consciousness 40
    of spirits 5
    see *also* spiritual evolution
exercise 69
expenditures, allocating for Spiritist Centers 100
extra-sensory perception 49

F

FDA *see* Food and Drug Administration
FDA approved drugs ix
FEB *see* Federation of Brazilian Spiritists
Federation of Brazilian Spiritists (FEB) vii,
    10, 17
    founding of 23
Federation of Brazilian Spiritists of San Paulo
    (FEESP) 10, 24, 25, 89–93, 107, 133
    classes available at 91
    drug addiction, treatment of 90–92
    mediumship training 89
    origins of 122
    School for Mediumship at 24, 92
    services provided by 89–90
feelings, negative 41, 42
fees for services viii, xii, 6–7, 134
    at Busca Vida 70
    at Centro 80
    for Hospice care 13
    mediums 32, 114
    Spiritualists 32
    sliding scale 13
    in USA ix
FEESP *see* Federation of Brazilian Spiritists
    of San Paulo
fields of life *see* energy fields
Fifteen Anathemas 148
    text of 152–154
Fifth Ecumenical Church Council 148
Filho, Arnold Marcondes 60
financial resources of Spiritist Centers 98–101
Fiscal Council, at Centro 97
focus 42, 87, 96
Food and Drug Administration (FDA) xi, 127
    regulations 126
    requirements of xi

forgiveness, in spiritual evolution 36, 107
Fox, Margaretta and Kate 30
fraternities 121–123
    spiritual 122
    in USA 123
Fraternity of the Disciples of Jesus 24, 25,
    92, 114, 122
Fraternity of the Four Leaf Clover 122
Fraternity of the Liberators 125
free clinics, Spiritist Centers as 3

G

Gates Foundation, Bill and Melinda xiii
General Assembly, at Centro 97
Genesis 21
genius 44
geo-magnetic energies 63, 68
God
    ability to speak to 21
    in the Basic Course 104
    belief in by those who attend Spiritist
    Centers 4, 83
    and Emotional level 42
    and healing 63
    and Integrated Personality level 45
    and Mental level 43
    paranormal powers in relationship with 6
    personal connection with 7, 107
    and Physical level 41
    and religion 32
    sense of the presence of 5
    and Spiritism 34
    spiritual experience with viii
God's Spirit, Spiritism as knowledge of 21
Goodheart, George 38
Gospel as Explained by Spiritist Doctrine,
    The 21, 26, 27, 28, 31, 104, 105, 108
gratitude, in spiritual evolution 36
Grobler, Johann 61
Group Confucius 22
guided imagery xii
Guirdam, Arthur 92

H

Hahneman, Samuel 22
Haley, Dan x
Hawkins, David x
    levels of consciousness 38
    levels of spiritual evolution, 38–49
    and muscle-testing 74

healers
    training for xii, 103–118
    trust in 87
    working in teams 6
healing
    AIDS viii, 4
    addiction see recovery from addiction
    cancer see cancer
    community and 76
    compulsions 8
    and electromagnetic devices 12, 67, 69
    emotional disorders 8
    geo-magnetic energies 63
    lifestyle affecting 69
    mental illness 19
    magnetic 22
    obsessions 8
    ovarian cancer viii
    pain viii
    positive outlook and 63, 69
    re-orientation 64
    schizophrenia viii, 60–61
    spiritual component of xii
    in Spiritist Centers 4
    stimulating with energy 10
    suicidal feelings 9, 90, 92, 133
    work in Levels of Initiation 46
health
    and positive attitude 48, 72
health care costs
    in USA x
    in Kardecist Spiritist Centers xii
    spiritual component of xii
health care, preventive xii
health care system, USA ix, x
health insurance
    cost of in USA x
heart patients xii
heaven
    and Emotional level of spiritual
    evolution 42
    as a psychological state vii
    questions about 83
Heaven and Hell 21
hell
    and Emotional level of spiritual
    evolution 42
    and Physical level of spiritual evolution 41
    as a psychological state vii
    questions about 83
herbal remedies xi, xii
Hess, David vii, 22, 127
Higher Self 46

homeopaths 22
Homeopathy 22
hope 75, 77, 87
Hospice 13
hospitals, and Spiritist Centers 96
How Cancer is a Point of Transformation 86
hyperactivity 86
hypnosis 112

I

illness, and Mental level of spiritual evolution 44
immune system, strengthening 74
incorporation 62
infant mortality rate in USA ix
inner transformation 31, 62, 87, 90
Inns and Innkeepers, Palmelo 64
Insanity Though a New Prism 23
intuition 49, 87, 112
    and mission 45
    as a sense 69
    see also medical intuition
insurance, cost of health x
Integrated Personality level 38, 44–45
interviews, personal 7
intuition, medical 5
    as a component of Homeopathy 22
invocation 50
IQ 44

J

JAMA see Journal of the American Medical
    Association
John of God viii, 4, 6, 128
Journal of the American Medical Association
    (JAMA) ix, xi
Jurriaanse, Aart 33, 38, 39, 45, 50
Justinian 147

K

Kardec, Allan vii, 19, 27
    doctrine of vii, 27
    texts used for courses 9
    books written by 20–21
Kardec philosophy 5
    study of xiii
Kardecismo see Spiritism
Kardecist see Kardec, Allan
Kardecist Spiritist Centers vii, xii, 3
    anonymity in xiv, 6, 17
    beliefs forming 5–7

Kardecist Spiritist Centers cont.
    budgets for 100–101
    building blocks of 95–96
    Casa de Dom Inácio vii
    classes available at 103–118
    donations to 6, 95, 98–99, 100 134
    evolving 14
    fees for services in viii, 6, 32, 80, 134
    financial resources of 98–101, 134
    maintenance of 4
    mission of 134
    models of 131–135
    as not-for-profit organizations 98
    number in Brazil 17
    organizational structure of 97–98
    physical layout of 7
    physical needs of 134
    raising money for 98–100
    religions, models for new 50
    restrictions in creating 126
    social events in 7
    starting outside of Brazil 95–96,
       121–129, 134–135
training at xii, 103–118
    typical activities in 7–10
Kardecist Spiritism *see* Spiritism
karma vii, 5, 19, 43, 96
kinesiology 38
    see also muscle-testing
Kirlian photography 112
Krucoff, Mitchell xii

L

Lakhovsky, Georges 75
Lang, Cosmo, Archbishop of Canterbury 21
Laussac, Paul 67–68, 72–76
Law of Progress 26
Lawlis, Frank 12
laying-on of hands 8
    and Edgard Armond 24
    energy medicine, form of 10
    see also energy passes
Le Shan, Lawrence 86
leadership, future of Kardecist Spiritism 25
legal advice, at Centro 79, 84
legal issues 126
levels of consciousness 38–39
    elevated by PT 72
    and mediumship 112
    see also levels of spiritual evolution
Levels of Initiation 45–48

levels of spiritual evolution 38–49
    Emotional 41–42
    of Initiation 45–48
    Integrated Personality 44–45
    Mental 43–44
    Physical 40–41
Liberation 113
libraries in Spiritist Centers 10
lifestyle, affect on healing 69
Lord's Prayer 59
love 106
    and Emotional level 41
    focus on 63
    in spiritual evolution 36
    unconditional 49
Lucas, Winafred 92
Luiz, Andre 23, 112, 113
Lupus 74

M

Macumba 22
magnetic fields
    relignment of 73
    treatment with 11
magnetic healing 112
    as a component of Homeopathy 22
Magnetic Portal 73
manic-depressive disorder, healing viii
Marcondes, Marcel Teles 60
massage therapy xi
Masters 46, 50, 76
materialism, path of (diagram) 36
Medicaid xii
medical consultations, at Centro 82
medical diagnoses, non-invasive 5
    see also medical intuition
medical intuition 5, 49
    at Palmelo 58–59
medical intuitives xiv, 8, 56
medical licenses, requirement for 126
medical problems, perceiving 5
Medicare xii
medication *see* drugs, prescription
medicine of the future *see* Energy Medicine
mediums 5
    annual reviews of 114
    and automatic writing 8–9
    at Centro 79, 87
    Christian 21
    electromagnetic devices, comparison
      with 74

mediums cont.
    fees for services 32
    at FEESP 89, 91
    Kardec's exploration of 21
    spirit communication through vii, 20
    training *see* School for Mediumship
    in USA 113
    teams 6
    see also mediumship
Mediums' Book, The 21, 61, 111
meditation 8, 13
    and healing 69
    and brotherhood 76
    health improved though xii
    and Levels of Initiation 46
Mediumship 24, 111
mediumship 3, 21
    with animals 111
    and Edgard Armond 24
    of Christ 111
    and mission 110
    religions 22
    scientific validation of 96
    training for 6, 89, 109, 110–115
    see also mediums
Memorial Sloan-Kettering Cancer Center xi
Menezes, Bezerra de 23
mental health, and positive attitude 48
mental illnesses
    spiritual causes of 23
Mental level 38, 43–44, 109
mentors 118–119, 124
metaphysics vii
Mind 43, 44
mission 109
    and intuition 45
    and mediumship 110
    of Spiritist Centers 134
    and teaching 116
Mosby's Alternative and Complementary
    Medicine: A Research Based
    Approach 12
Moses 21
Mosquera, Martin 25
mortality *see* death
muscle-testing 38–39, 74
music
    expositions, in Spiritist Centers 10
    and lower death rates xii
Myrna Brind Center at Thomas Jefferson
    Hospital xi
mysticism 6

N

Nag Hammadi Scrolls 150
National Cancer Institute xi
National Foundation for Alternative Medicine
    (NFAM) x, xi
National Institutes of Health xi, 72
Natural Laws
    in Basic Course 105
    at Mental level 43
negatively-motivated spirits *see* spirits
new physics vii
new religions 50
New Testament 90, 146
NFAM *see* National Foundation for
    Alternative Medicine
non-Western treatments *see* alternative
    healthcare or complementary health-
    care
not-for-profit organizations, Spiritist Centers
    as 98
nutrition, and healing 69

O

obsession *see* spirit obsession
Oneness 47
orixas 22
Oschman, James 10, 11, 76
out of the body 23
outreach, community 90, 101
Oxford Dictionary of World Religions, The 32

P

Pagels, Elaine 150
pain
    as an alarm clock 65
    healing viii
    management and treatment off 11–12
    and Mental level of spiritual evolution 44
Palmelo, Brazil viii, 55–66, 132
Parable of the Sower 109
paranormal 6, 24, 30, 49, 109, 113
parapsychology vii, 19
    Hernani Guimaraes Andrade 24
Passes and Radiaçoes: Metodos Espiritas de
    Cura 24
Pastoral Counselors 126
Pauling, Linus xii, 38
peace, focus on 63
Pelosi, Nancy 95
penal code, Brazil 22, 92

perfection, as goal of spiritual evolution 45, 91, 105

peri-spirit 104, 108, 110

personal consultations 8

personal interviews 7–8

personal transformation
as cure for emotional problems 23
and healing 45
and Spiritualism 31

pharmacy, Centro 79, 82, 100

Phenomenon of Spiritism, The 112

Phillipines, popularity of Spiritism in 17

Philosophical Studies 23

physical bodies
transmitting energy to 12

physical health, and positive attitude 48

Physical level 38, 40–41

physical nerve plexes 110

physics, new vii

physics, theoretical and Levels of Initiation 47

Pineal Trainer (PT) 72
and positive thoughts 73

Planeta viii

Planning Council, at Centro 97

poltergeist 113

poor, the x, 14, 18
help provided by Spiritists Centers for xii, 9
homeopaths helping 22
support provided by Centro for 79–86, 108

positive attitude 48, 63, 69, 72, 77

Posthumous Works 21

poverty, in Brazil 14

Powell, L. H. xii

Power versus Force: An Anatomy of Consciousness x, 38, 74

powers, paranormal 6

prayer xii, 13, 69
in the Basic Course 104
Christian 8
health improved though xii
and Levels of Initiation 46
in Spiritist Centers 4, 8, 14, 32

Prayer of the Fraternities 125

pre-embodiment *see* reincarnation

pregnancy, care at Centro 82

premonitions 5

prescription drugs
cost of ix
and Centro pharmacy 79, 82
research of xi

prevention of disease states 11

preventive
health care xii
medicine 80

Problem of Being, Destiny and Suffering, The 112

Protestant theology vii

psychic surgery iv
at Abadiania 133
at Palmelo 56, 57, 58, 63, 132

psychoanalysis 23

psychokinesis 20, 30, 113

psychometry 112

psychosomatic component of disease 86

PT *see* Pineal Trainer

purification, for inner transformation 90

Q

Quantum Vibrational Therapy (QVT) 75 -76

Quimbanda 22

QVT *see* Quantum Vibrational Therapy

R

Radin, Dean 151

records, in Spiritist Centers 6, 17, 100

recovery from addiction vii, 9, 64, 72, 90–92

re-embodiment *see* reincarnation

reforma intima 45, 62

Reiki 67
energy passes, compared with 91
taught in the USA 128
see also laying-on of hands

reincarnation vii, 5, 18, 19, 96
and Christianity 145–155
Ian Stevenson's research of 24
and Spiritism 30, 107
and Spiritualism 31

rejuvenation devices *see* electromagnetic devices

religion
definitions of 32–33
and Emotional level of spiritual evolution 42
and God 32
and Integrated Personality level 45
and Mental level of spiritual evolution 43
need for new 50
and Physical level of spiritual evolution 41
relationship with science 19
Spiritism as 34, 85, 107
Spiritism, comparison with 32–34

Religions of Man, The 32
remission of symptoms viii
remuneration *see* fees for services
re-orientation 64, 66, 77, 112
research
    alternative health protocols xiii
    biophysics and cellular biology 10
    cancer 75
    cost of ix, xi
    electrostimulators 72
    magnetic fields for treatment 11
    medical 11
    mediumship 96
    muscle-testing 39
    parapsychology 19
    Quantum Vibrational Therapy (QVT) 76
    trans-cranial electro-stimulation 72
reviews
    of mediums 114
    of teachers 117
Rife, Royal 75
Right Action 49
Rivail, Hippolyte *see* Kardec. Allan
Roy, Rustum xiii
Russia, and electromagnetic devices 72

S

Salu 64
Samba in the Night 22
San Paulo
    Brazilian Federation of Spiritists of (FEESP) 89–93
    Centro 79
    Federation of Brazilian Spiritists(FEB) vii
schizophrenic *see* schizophrenia
schizophrenia
    healing of viii, 60–61
    causes of 62
School for Mediumship, at FEESP 24, 92, 104, 122, 124
Schwartz, Gary 111, 151
science, modern vii
    relationship with religion 20
séances 30, 33
Secretary, class 116–117
self-awareness, development of 40
service work 49
    and Spiritism 19, 28, 32, 34
    and Integrated Personality level 45
    and Levels of Initiation 45
    and Mental level 45

at Palmelo 64, 65
    and Right Action 49
shamanic tradition in Brazil 18
shamans, similarity to Spiritists 18
Silva Mind Control 67
skill building courses, in Spiritist Centers 9
Smith, Huston 32
social events, in Spiritist Centers 7
socialized medicine, in Brazil 18
Souls 45, 47
    in Basic Course 104
    infused 40, 43
    survives death 19, 21
soup kitchens, at Spiritist Centers 3, 89, 108
Speeden, Leila 90
spirit communication 20
    first recorded in USA 30
spirit obsession 8, 59, 90, 113
    as cause of mental illness 23
    and electromagnetic devices 69
    and negative patterns in the mind 62
    see also dis-obsession
    see also and de-possession
Spiritism vii, 1, 5–7
    banned by Brazil's penal code 22, 92
    charity in 34
    and children 107
    demographics of 17
    and God 34
    history of 17–27
    Holy Spirit communicating as 21
    and laws of cause and effect 30
    leadership of 25
    and New Testament 90
    organizational style of 31–32
    religion, comparison with 32–34, 85
    Spiritualism, comparison with 29–32
    study and good work for 30
    universal principles (truths) 4, 5
Spiritist Center of Light and Truth 56
Spiritist Centers *see* Kardecist Spiritist Centers
Spiritists vii
    similarity to shamans 18
    reaction to religious repression 22
    see also Spiritism
spirit-rapping *see* psychokinesis
spirits 19
    attachment 8
    highly developed 5
    negatively motivated 8
    see also disincarnates

Spirits and Scientists 127
Spirits' Book, The 20, 22, 61, 104–105, 111
*Spiritual Alliances: Discovering the Roots of
Health at the Casa de Dom Inácio* viii
Spiritual community centers vii
spiritual development *see* spiritual evolution
spiritual evolution vii, xii, xiv, 37–49, 64–65
    acceleration of vii, 5, 45
    and the Basic Course 104, 105
    charity in 19
    discipline in 7
    Emotional level of 41–42, 109
    empowering 45–46
    and extra-sensory perception 49
    goal of Spiritist Centers 3
    good works 30
    groups, need for new to facilitate 50
    of humanity 45, 46
    Integrated Personality Level of 44
    levels of 38–49
    Levels of Initiation of 45–48
    map of 34
    Mental level of 43–44
    and paranormal abilities 49
    pace of 40
    path of 35
    perfection 45, 91
    permeable boundaries of 39
    Physical level of 40–41
    qualities of 36
    of societies 38
    study 30
    volition 39
spiritual experiences viii
spiritual healing centers, Spiritist Centers as 3
spiritual healing, importance of xiv
spiritual illness 23
spiritual path (diagram) 35
Spiritualism 29
    indwelling spirit 31
    investigated by Cosmo Lang 21
    charity 31
    consistency with Christianity 21
    organizational style of 31–32
    reincarnation 31
    Spiritism, comparison with 29–32
    see also Spiritualists
Spiritualists
    fees for services 32
    see also Spiritualism
SQUID (Superconducting Quantum
    Interference Device) 11–12

statistics gathered at Centro 82
Stevenson, Ian 24, 151
stress 48
    and cancer 86
study, and spiritual development 30
subtle bodies *see* subtle energy bodies
subtle energy bodies 8, 57, 108
    transmitting energy to 12
subtle energy fields 61, 110
suicide 90
Superconducting Quantum Interference
    Device *see* SQUID
surgery 11, 12, 65, 133
    and curandeirismo law 128
    and electromagnetic devices 69
    see also psychic surgery
symptoms viii, 8
synagogues 13

T

table moving *see* psychokinesis
T'ai Chi 67, 68, 76
TCES *see* trans-cranial electro-stimulator
teachers
    annual reviews of 117
    finding outside Brazil 118–119
    preparation for 116–118
    training for 103–118
teams, healers or mediums working in 6
telepathy 49, 112, 113
Theodora 147
therapeutic touch xii, 128
Thomas Jefferson Hospital, Myrna Brind
    Center at xi
Thomaz, Martha Gallego 25, 80, 122, 125
Thymus Gland Activator 74
Tibetan, the *see* DK
touch, therapeutic xii, 128
training
    advanced students, in Spiritist Centers 9
    as a class Secretary 116–117
    healers xiii, 103–118
    to give energy passes 115–116
    teachers 116–118
trans-cranial electro-stimulator (TCES) 72
translations, problems with 27
trauma medicine 11
treatment *see* healing
trust, in healers 87

U

Umbanda 22, 33
Underhill, Evelyn 6
UNESCO 56
United Nations Educational, Scientific and
    Cultural Organization *see* UNESCO
United States of America (USA)
    cost of health care in ix
    economic situation, current 95
    health care system in ix–xii
    infant mortality rate in ix
    mediums in 113–114
    resources for spiritual inspiration and
    evolution 13
    spirit-communication, first recorded 30
    Spiritists Centers in 123
    spiritual fraternities in 123
    war on cancer ix, xii, 75
universal truths in Spiritism 5
USA *see* United States of America

V

Vice President's Cancer Panel Meeting ix
vital fluids vii
volition, and spiritual evolution 39
volunteering xii, 65, 80, 117
    see also charity

W

war on cancer, USA ix, xii, 10
welfare systems, Spiritist Centers as 3
WHO *see* World Health Organization
work and study, in Spiritism 30
World Above, The 112
World Health Organization (WHO) ix

X

Xavier, Chico 23, 25, 96, 111, 113
    and electromagnetic devices 75
    texts used for courses 9

Y

yoga 13, 67, 68, 76

Grateful acknowledgement is made to:

Veritas Publishing to quote David Hawkins, MD,
Power vs Force: An Anatomy of Consiousness, © 1995.
Veritas Publishing, 151 Keller Lane, Sedona, Arizona.

Johann Grobler, MD, to quote from *Bridges, and Prophecies*,
by Aart Jurriaanse

The Allan Kardec Educational Society, to quote from
The Gospel Explained by the Spiritist Doctrine, © 2000.
Philadelphia, PA.

About the Author:

 Emma Bragdon, PhD. is the author of three other books on the relationship between spiritual evolution and health. Her first two books, *The Call of Spiritual Emergency* and *A Sourcebook for Helping People with Spiritual Problems*, helped professionals and laypeople discern the differences between phenomena of spiritual awakening and symptoms of mental disease. Since 2001 Dr. Bragdon has been visiting Spiritist Centers in Brazil to understand more about the spiritual and physical healing that takes place there. Having introduced "John of God" to the international community through her book, *Spiritual Alliances: Discovering the Roots of Health at the Casa de Dom Inacio*, she is now working on a book about Paul Laussac's electromagnetic devices for healing.

Dr. Bragdon travels frequently between New England, Brazil and South Africa. She is a guide for tours to the Casa de Dom Inácio, where participants consult with world-renowned "John of God."

www.emmabragdon.com
www.spiritualalliances.com
EBragdon@aol.com